CHAR

As I travel the country, I a [illegible] in this nation awakening from its [illegible]p. The alarm call is from God to proclaim the Good News to the lost and damaged people of our schools and universities, our factories, offices and shops, our communities and our cities. In this book that alarm call rings clear. Nick Cuthbert's driving conviction is that God is rousing us to spend our lives introducing people to Jesus. It is practical, incisive, stimulating and positive.

—***J. John***
Director, The Philo Trust

Nick Cuthbert's writing is refreshing and full of common sense. He is an evangelist with a pastor's heart and rooted in his local church. We would all do well to listen to what he has to say.

—***Lyndon Bowring***
Director, Care Trust

As always, Nick has something very important to say to the church in this country.

—***Nicky Gumbel***
Holy Trinity Brompton, London

This book is much needed, long overdue and heartily welcomed. It will help restore evangelism to its proper place in our church's programme. I heartily recommend it.

—***Wynne Lewis***
General Superintendent, Foursquare Gospel Alliance

World evangelism is high on the agenda of the world church. Nick Cuthbert's heart cry pleads, promises, warns and exhorts us to get it on to the agenda of the church in the UK before we miss out. He does it in a winsome way that makes us hungry for the reality. His message—urging the church to look out and move out—is on time. We must not get left behind!

—***Roger Forster***
Ichthus Fellowship, London

Charismatics in Crisis

Nick Cuthbert

KINGSWAY PUBLICATIONS
EASTBOURNE

First published 1994

ISBN 0 85476 452 6

Produced by Bookprint Creative Services
P.O. Box 827, BN21 3YJ, England for
KINGSWAY PUBLICATIONS LTD
Lottbridge Drove, Eastbourne, E Sussex BN23 6NT.
Printed in Great Britain

Contents

Introduction

I don't know if you are standing in a shop flicking through this book, wondering whether it is worth parting with your money, or you have actually said good-bye to some cash and got the book home. Either way, let me tell you why it has been written.

Some books are written to teach believers more about their faith or how to understand the Bible better. This is not one of those.

Some are written as biographies to inspire us with what God has done in someone else's life. I love those books, but this is not one of them.

Some books are written to give to people who are not yet Christians. This not one of those either.

This is one person's heart cry for the church in the West not to miss the open door that it is currently being presented with. It is an encouragement for us to get back to our original purpose and put secondary issues aside. It is written in the belief that God has given us promises that if we obey him, we will see fruit for our labours. It is written at a time when the press and media are telling us that everything is going downhill as far as the church is concerned. But it is a time when those who have eyes to see are seeing very green shoots beginning to appear everywhere. It is a time of hope.

But it is also about a warning. A warning that is not, in the main, being heeded—the consequences of which are a church torn apart by strife and tension. We are a church that has left itself wide open to both God's judgement and the enemy's work.

There are two distinct parts to this book. One part needs the other. I hope that something in it will spur us all on to be part of what God wants to do through his church.

A PROMISE

Be strong and courageous, because you will lead these people to inherit the land I swore to their forefathers to give them. *Be strong and very courageous*. Be careful to obey all the law my servant Moses gave you; do not turn from it to the right or to the left, that you may be successful wherever you go. Do not let this Book of the Law depart from your mouth; meditate on it day and night, so that you may be careful to do everything written in it. Then you will be prosperous and successful. Have I not commanded you? *Be strong and courageous*. Do not be terrified; do not be discouraged, for the Lord your God will be with you wherever you go (Josh 1:6-9, italics mine).

All authority in heaven and on earth has been given to me. Therefore go and make disciples of all nations, baptising them in the name of the Father and of the Son and of the Holy Spirit and teaching them to obey everything I have commanded you. *And surely I am with you always, to the very end of the age* (Mt 28:18-20, italics mine).

1

The Spirit of the Lord Is upon Me

Today we are facing a crisis. It is, in fact, a moment of opportunity, but an opportunity itself creates a crisis. Moments of opportunity nearly always require change; change requires choice and choices produce crisis—particularly when it is perceived that something could be lost. The proverbial monkey who has put his hand into the jar to grab the peanut is faced with a crisis. To let go of the peanut means he may lose it. To hold on to it may mean he will lose his life, as he's hindered by the jar around his hand. The man who wants to invest his money in a project faces a crisis. He stands to gain, but in doing so could lose everything he has. Choices produce crisis. The church faces a crisis that it cannot afford to ignore. To ignore it may seem the comfortable option, but it is the route to utter irrelevancy and death. To take up the challenge may cost everything, but it could lead to the salvation of a nation.

This crisis is, or certainly should be, felt particularly in the charismatic wing of the church. Unfortunately, that may well be the part that is most oblivious to any problems because the life that does exist may hide the fundamental problem within. Those of us who put ourselves in that category, and all those who claim to believe in the power and presence of the Holy Spirit, must ask ourselves the question, 'What is the evidence of an authentic move of the Holy Spirit?' Then we need to look at what we have seen in this country over the last thirty years and ask whether what we have seen and experienced fits this description. Have we really seen an effective work of the Spirit in the church or have we allowed ourselves to come short of what could have been and could still be? Is there any possibility that we have settled for something less than God intended, and are we in any way responsible for that?

When we look at the life of Jesus, it is very striking that as soon as the Holy Spirit came upon him he was thrust out into a time of conflict with the powers of darkness. When his time in the wilderness was over, he went immediately out into the world preaching the good news of the kingdom. Then for three years he consistently preached about the kingdom of God, healed the sick and demonstrated the reality of this kingdom. In Luke 4:18-19, we read that he said of himself: 'The Spirit of the Lord is on me because he has anointed me to preach good news to the poor. He has sent me to proclaim freedom for the prisoners and recovery of sight for the blind, to release the oppressed, to proclaim the year of the Lord's favour.' Here, he gives us a clear indication of the work of the Holy Spirit, not only in his life, but in the life, of what was to be the church.

The anointing of the Holy Spirit was given so that the world could be touched by the love and the power of God. Although individual Christians would be blessed by the coming of the Holy Spirit, the supreme work of the Spirit was not to stop with individuals, but to embrace the world outside. When Jesus talked about the Spirit of God, upon him, he did so in terms of the effect it would have on an unbelieving world. The Holy Spirit came upon Jesus so that he could bring healing, restoration and deliverance. In the same way the Holy Spirit has come on the church, not primarily for itself, but for a lost world.

Later, on the Day of Pentecost when the Holy Spirit filled those early disciples, we see an immediate and similar response. First of all there was strong praise and a gathering of large crowds of people. Then, almost immediately, it was followed by preaching and a massive response to the gospel. The rest of the Acts of the Apostles is a continuation of this same work. The Spirit empowered disciples to go everywhere preaching the good news. This eventually led to Paul's missionary journeys and the start of the churches in so many different towns and cities.

The coming of the Spirit caused an explosion of evangelism across the known world.

Of course, as we read in Acts 2 and Acts 4, there were many other works of the Holy Spirit that affected the church. There was the building of committed fellowship together; the sharing of financial resources; the sense of community; the gifts of the Holy Spirit; the release of ministries and an understanding of the body of Christ. There were these and many other indications of the Holy Spirit at work, but supremely there was an explosion of power which touched unbelievers.

As we look at worldwide revivals throughout church history as well as today, we see that wherever the Holy Spirit has come in power, the result has been large numbers of people coming into the kingdom of God. We would have to conclude from all of this that the central work of the Spirit is not only to bring the presence of God to the hearts of believers, but to move through them to touch the world and reveal Jesus. If we were to look at charismatic renewal today in the West, we would have to say that we have gained many of the attributes of the post-Pentecost experience. The Holy Spirit has made Jesus real to us, taught us his word, assured us of the Father's love, and enabled us to show his fruit. We've come into a realisation of what it is to be the body of Christ. We've discovered a certain degree of unity. We have certainly found fresh understanding and experience of the gifts of the Holy Spirit, a release in worship and new songs, and to some extent the evidence of the miraculous, but we would have to say in the midst of all this that we have barely touched the world. This is in stark contrast to so much of the Pentecostal movement worldwide. There are clearly many factors that may make a nation more or less open to the gospel, but certainly there does have to be the heart and desire within the church for the Spirit to work in this way.

I'm not for a moment suggesting that what we have experienced has not been an authentic work of the Holy Spirit, but we would have to say that it has been incomplete. Surely this cannot be a lack on the part of the Holy Spirit of God, for he cannot possibly have changed his purpose in coming. We need to look at ourselves and see whether, in recent years, there have been areas where we have failed to allow the Holy Spirit to achieve what he wanted, and have instead turned his work in upon ourselves.

This is not a time for guilt and navel-gazing, but it is a time for being honest with ourselves and for seeing how we can now change. We could be on the verge of another great outpouring of the Holy Spirit, but he may be waiting for us to be facing in the right direction. What would be the point of the wind blowing strongly if the ship was in harbour with no intention of leaving?

These questions not only face those who call themselves charismatic, but also all those who could be labelled evangelicals. We have seen, particularly in the Church of England, a growth in the number of evangelical leaders, which is certainly a wonderful and very positive thing. For some time there has been an increased emphasis on preaching the word and an understanding of the need for conversion, and yet research suggests that church attendance in many places has been declining. This is true of evangelical churches as well as others. Again we have to ask some very fundamental questions of ourselves.

If we look at the subject matter of many of our conferences over the last few years, so much has to do with things that affect the church. Even healing and deliverance, which always bring out the crowds, are so often attractive to people who want to learn about these subjects to help themselves. To go to a conference on 'How to win my neighbour for Jesus' seems far less attractive than 'Knowing how to receive inner healing'. Of course, in a world of so many broken lives, we need to see as much healing as possible, but so much of what we do is rooted primarily in a desire to serve ourselves. We eagerly await the next international ministry which will give us more thrills than the last one.

Going round in circles

The point was illustrated to me quite graphically when I went to visit some people who lived in a house in the north of England. I was woken in the middle of the night by a terrible whirring sound. I got up and looked around the room, but couldn't find the source of this noise, and yet it was too irritating to ignore and just go back to bed. So I went out onto the landing and I saw a little hamster in a cage. It was rushing round on a small wheel at an enormous rate and at the same time making quite a noise. I tried to quieten the thing down and explained that it oughtn't to be doing this in the middle of the night! But it ignored me and seemed intent on continuing its relentless journey. Eventually, having failed to push it off the wheel, I went back into my room, fetched a biro and jammed it in the wheel. The hamster gave me such a look. I've never forgotten it and I've always wanted to go back and say sorry! Nevertheless, it had the desired effect, as the hamster scuttled back into its fluff and appeared to go to sleep.

I'm sure many of us have had similar experiences and can visualise the energy used by the little animals as they rush around in circles going nowhere but certainly getting plenty of excercise. It reminds me so much of our church activity. We find ourselves going round the same way over and over again, wondering why we haven't made a great deal of progress. It may be time to stop and ask fundamental questions about where we are going, if anywhere.

Some of the young people in our church raised quite a lot of money recently by cycling from the North to the South Pole. What they did was to gather fifteen exercise bikes into one room and over the period of a weekend cycle non-stop the same number of miles as going Pole to Pole! They worked very hard and were certainly much fitter at the end of it and had raised money for charity. It is quite extraordinary to think that they never even left the room while cycling 11,000 miles.

With all our church busyness and activity; with all our committees and meetings; with all the expertise that we now have—it is vitally important for us to stop and take stock. Our activity could blind us to the fact that we are not actually going anywhere. We must always be asking the question whether we are actually achieving anything and whether, with all our know-how, we are any more effective in making an impact on our generation.

The Children of Israel wandered around the wilderness for forty years. They were never intended to do so. We are told that it was only two weeks' journey to the Jordan river and the edge of Canaan, but of course when they got there they failed to enter, and spent the entire time wandering round and round. It was a time of miracles. Day after day they got up and found manna on the ground.

What an amazing sight that must have been! They saw God miraculously provide water for them from a rock. This was a generation who saw the most wonderful acts of God's power. They knew his leading. A fire was with them by night and a cloud by day. They were very aware of the presence of God in their midst. These were not a people distant from God who did not know his power. And yet for all the miracles, all the presence of the living God; for all the manifestation of power, these people failed to enter into what God had for them.

Nowadays when people talk about this being 'the generation to go into the land', it can sound as if we are in some way special. The truth is that every individual and every generation has a promised land to take. There are things that God has prepared for us in our lives and we should want to come to the end of our life and know that we have finished the work he gave us to do.

But if we never stop and take stock, we may well not fulfil his greater purposes for us. This is a time when many people are beginning to ask fundamental questions about where we should be going and what our priorities should be.

The sad thing would be if we were to look at the outward signs of God's presence with us and assume that 'this is it' when in fact we are just doing another circuit of the wilderness. We are faced with a land that needs to be infiltrated with the gospel. There has got to be a systematic invasion.

Thankfully in many sectors of the church things are beginning to change, but it is going to take a large dose of courage and boldness for us to see the situation turned round.

Under orders

We are a people under orders. God wants a job done. On the cross Jesus broke the power of Satan and sent us out in his authority. He has given us his Spirit and now he sends us out with work to do. Our only response can be obedience. It is not dependent on our success or failure, or how we appear to get on, but we must be obedient to what we are shown.

For the church in the West this is a time of profound challenge. I also think it is a time of tremendous opportunity, not only for the church nationally but for every local church. The greatest danger is that the church will lose heart and pull back. When the world is in such tremendous need and is aware of its helplessness, the last thing we should do now is to hold back. The greatest danger for the church is that we will retreat instead of going forward, and so miss the opportunity of seeing God act on a scale that we have not yet experienced.

Building the church

God's instrument is still the local church. I rejoice with others in all the work mission organisations have achieved over recent years. Much of it has had to be done by such groups because the church has been so weak. Jesus said he would build the church. Paul gave his life to spreading the gospel across the known world but it was always to build the church. It is still Jesus' work today. It is the developing of strong interrelated local churches that will be both the instrument of warfare to oppose the powers of darkness and also the place of shelter and community for lost men and women.

What is meant by the local church may well have to take on new meaning. We no longer live in a rural environment of small towns and villages. It is the age of the city and the mobile population. For most people, their understanding of 'local' is varied. In Birmingham, where I live, their local football team is Aston Villa whose ground may be some distance away, whereas the local pub maybe less than a mile away. In the same way, the local church may well be both large and city-wide as well as small and locality-based. I do not think this would be far from the New Testament pattern.

It is also the day of the city church; not a monolithic uniting of all churches into one group, but a clear, committed working together of churches across a city to express the unity we already have in Christ, to unite in pulling down the strongholds of Satan and in bringing the gospel to every home. We can no longer afford the 'luxury' of being separate. When Paul wrote to the Ephesian church, he did not tell them to create unity but to maintain it. When we realise that in any given locality we are 'one church but many congregations', we are acknowledging the unity we already have, not trying to create something new. We are being alerted to the reality of what we are and the need to repent of our sinful and man-made divisions. If we want to express love for Jesus this is not an option it's a requirement. This is a time for the repairing of nets. Who knows how close we are to an enormous catch of fish? What an incalculable tragedy it would be if the nets were broken and many fish were lost. The rebuilding of nets must be a priority at this time as we seek to look out into the world. It will save us from being introverted into the 'my church' syndrome and mean we can bring in the great harvest. This requires a heart for unity and servanthood towards one another that has not been seen for a very long time.

There are some who say that it is therefore all right to belong to no one church in particular because we all belong to the wider body of Christ. This is usually an excuse for independence and a lack of accountability. In the early church, even if they were a city-wide church, everyone knew their place in belonging. To belong to 'the church in the city' must mean that you also belong to one of the bodies that make up that church. Everyone needs to belong to an identifiable, real body of people to whom they can be accountable and in which they can serve. This building of nets is the working together of those bodies. In Ezekiel's vision of bones, they came together to form bodies, lots of separate bodies, but the bodies formed together to make one army. What an army we could be if we would march together against a common enemy.

It is interesting to observe trends and see what the Spirit is doing. There seems to be a move across the world for churches to begin to find one another and serve one another in the greater work of impacting towns and cities with the gospel. Since we have failed so badly in the past in this area, it must be a work of God that is enabling it to happen today. There is cost in this. Any act of giving, serving, laying our lives and reputations down for others has got to be costly, but if it helps to honour God and bring in a vast harvest, it is worth it. Who really cares which boat is most full of fish? But how sad if the catch is lost because the fishermen would not work together.

I know that the easiest thing to do is to find an area of weakness and hammer it. In one sense any fool can do that. It's easy for a reasonable preacher to make people feel guilty over prayer, evangelism and many other things, because these are all areas where we are not as effective as we could or should be. Having been involved in evangelistic ministry for many years and seen a church planted and grow, I am aware of the pressure of people telling us that we could do more. I am also aware that yet another formula is not good enough. The more we press on, the more we see the need for revival and for God's sovereign intervention in our affairs if we are ever going to see a real change.

Having said that, and risking the feeling that we have been this way before, it is vital that we challenge one another, encourage one another and seek to help one another find ways to be relevant to our world. We will need to learn what it means to share ministry gifts between churches. Some are led by evangelists and some by pastors. I have often wondered whether the ministry gifts are found in what we term 'the local church', or whether the Lord has put a wide variety of gifted people into the church in a city or town because he wants us to learn to serve one another. The evangelist in one local church is able to help a neighbouring church. Similarly with teachers. This kind of co-operation certainly prevents insularity and helps the unity of the body in each place.

There must be a way of mutually benefiting from what God has put in the wider body so that we are all enriched. As long as our prime motivation remains solely to build our own church, it is unlikely we will be willing to share gifts and resources. A church working in the suburbs, full of middle-class, professional people will probably never be struggling financially. A church working among the poor with a high percentage of unemployed people will always struggle in terms of personal and material resources. To the onlooker, the answer to that situation is obvious—but how often does it ever happen? Maybe when we really see our job as working together to reach the town or city, things will change. When our sense of calling is to pastor a church, rather than reach a town, what other people are doing will be of casual interest or even seen as competition. But if we see our call as being to win a town to Christ, we will be more willing to share what God has given us.

I remember many years ago meeting with some other

ministers. The Lord brought a scene to my mind. It was of a group of parachutists, being dropped behind enemy lines. They were meant to land, regroup and begin to work together to find and fight the enemy. In fact they remained separate, and were so afraid and on edge that they began to fire on one another in an attempt to protect themselves. This picture is not a far cry from how we see one another today. How much more could we achieve together?

2

The Last Thing He Told Us to Do

If you have ever studied last words, you'll know that they fall into two categories: those which are intended and those which are unintended.

The unintended last words are often remembered for their humorous side. You can obtain books of famous last words like: 'It looks like a mushroom to me;' or, 'Who says it's unsafe'? or, 'Of course it's not loaded.' Those sorts of things are interesting, but not of world-shaking significance. But there are many last words that are intentional and because of the person who spoke them, are much more significant. These may be the last words spoken either at the end of someone's life or at a particular time before some major event, and given as a reminder to people of what is important.

These sorts of last words or instructions are significant because the person who speaks them wants you to take particular note of them.

I know that when my wife Lois goes away on a trip and I'm left at home to look after the house, I can tell exactly what her last words to me are going to be. I know she says things like, 'I love you, I'll be praying for you and thinking of you' – all those lovely things wives say to husbands and which I always appreciate. But I know what her *very* last words will be because they are always the same – 'Don't forget to water the plants!' She says it last because that's one of the things that are really important to her and she is keen for me not to forget. She also knows that I am likely to do just that unless she makes a special point of it.

We usually have a major panic just before she returns and we've seen some great miracles in resurrections of plants!

As a child you may remember hearing the words, 'What was the last thing I told you to do?' and certainly those of us who are parents will have said them.

You know what it's like; you're going out for the evening and you've forgotten to take in the washing, so you say to the children, 'Whatever you do, please do not forget to get the washing in.'

You get in later and you ask, 'Why is the washing still on the line? It has rained and now everything is wet again.'

They tell you enthusiastically, and as if they have not heard your question, that they have at least cleaned the dishes.

'What was the last thing I told you to do?'

'We've also cleared the living room.'

'What was the last thing I told you to do? Why do you think I bothered to ask you? Because the washing needed to come in, and now it is too late.'

If we put great store on our last words in situations, then how much more attention should we be giving to the last words of Jesus. Of course, God did not stop speaking 2,000 years ago, but the last instructions of Jesus here on earth must be of immense importance, and we would be foolish to ignore them.

If you were to assume that the church is now doing the last thing Jesus told us to do and you didn't know what those last words were, then by looking at the church what would you conclude his last words had been? You could be forgiven for assuming that the last thing Jesus said was: 'When I return, I want to find a church that is ready. I want your relationships to be good. I want your worship to be exciting. I want you to learn to minister to one another. I want you to live holy lives. That's the sort of church I'm coming back for. Those are the things you are to concentrate on.'

Now those are all good things and they are things Jesus taught, so we must do them. But it wasn't the last thing. It wasn't the thing that he underlined to his followers. He actually taught the importance of listening to instructions. He told parables about land owners who went away and left the servants to carry on things and when they came back they expected to find their servants doing the thing they were asked to do. In other words, I believe Jesus was saying, 'When I come back I want to find you active in the thing that I asked you to do.' I wonder what I would say if God were to stand in front of me today and say, 'Nick, what was the last thing I asked you, as part of my church, to do?'

I might well begin, 'Well, well I....'

'The last thing, Nick, the last thing, the very last thing.'

'We're doing a lot of good things. We have house groups, good worship. You know, we have four worship bands now, Lord.'

The Lord might say, 'What was the last thing I asked you to do?'

'By the way, Lord, we've got plans for this, that and the other. We're very busy.'

'What was the last thing I told you to do?'

Intentional last words are very important because they are the thing that the person wants you to remember. The intentional last words of Jesus are incredibly important.

If you look at the last instructions of Jesus, you will find that they are totally consistent with the whole of Scripture.

The message that runs right through Scripture is that God intervenes in his world to reach and to rescue men and women. As you read the New Testament, you find in the Gospels that the central theme of Jesus' teaching and ministry is that God loves the world and he wants to reach men and women. Isn't that what he is saying in the stories of the Prodigal Son, the lost coin, and the lost sheep? Isn't he saying that God desperately cares about lost people? The central theme of Jesus' teaching is that the Father cares about lost people? The story of the lost son intimates that the Father is always looking for prodigals to return. Why should Jesus have told us that the father saw him 'while he was a long way off' if he didn't want to tell us something of his Father's continuing search for rebellious people wanting to come home? How fantastic if we can help in that process. We couldn't be nearer understanding the heart of God than that. If it were not true, it makes a nonsense of the cross. It also makes a nonsense of the Acts of the Apostles and the rest of church history.

What is the central theme of Jesus' life? Yes, he gathered his disciples and taught them, but the continuing theme of the Gospels is that Jesus looked out on the crowds of people and had compassion on them. The centre of his life was that he cared about people who had no relationship with God. The focus of his teaching was that God's heart is always reaching out to those who do not know him. Why did he go to the cross? So that sinful people could be saved. Why did he send his Holy Spirit? So that the church could know him and be empowered to reach lost people with good news.

Jesus said that the Spirit of the Lord was upon him because he had anointed him to do what? To preach good news; to proclaim freedom, recovery of sight, release for the oppressed and the acceptable year of the Lord. All of the things the Spirit of God came upon Jesus to do were for the world. They were for lost people. The whole theme of Scripture and the New Testament is that God cares about people not yet in the kingdom. It is the deep longing of God that none should be lost. If you know God in any way at all, you will find that you have a concern for lost people. That has been the dynamic motivation of the church since its earliest days.

Final instructions

The last words of Jesus are consistent in at least three of the gospel accounts. Matthew and Mark record almost identical words, and Luke picks up the same theme in a different form. It is undoubtedly true that what was on the heart of Jesus before he left this earth was to send the disciples out with the commission to reach the world with the good news of salvation.

At the end of Matthew's Gospel Jesus said, 'All authority in heaven and on earth has been given to me. Therefore go and make disciples of all nations, baptising them in the name of the Father and of the Son and of the Holy Spirit, and teaching them to obey everything I have commanded you.'

There are three commands in this passage. The word 'go' is not a command. In the original Greek it means 'having gone'. Jesus assumes that everybody will be going. After all, we're always going somewhere. In other words, he says, 'In your going—having gone to work, having gone out for the evening, having gone home, having gone—make disciples, baptise them, and teach them to obey.' Three simple commands that he gives to us: make disciples, baptise and teach to obey. Then, he adds some wonderful words of encouragement that, as we go, he is with us always, even to the end of the age.

In our own church we wanted to put the mission that

God had given us into a clear phrase so that we knew what our prime calling was. We decided on: 'To help non-Christian people become obedient disciples of Jesus.' It might be different for different churches, but the theme should be the same and everyone should know what it is.

Wouldn't it be fantastic if someone were to ask the question of any Christian, 'What is the vision of the church of which you are a part?' and the reply was, 'To help non-Christian people become obedient disciples of Jesus,' or words to that effect? If you take a stick of rock (the kind you eat) and cut it in the middle, it has the same message all the way through. Wouldn't it be great if you took any Christian at random in the church and asked them to state the vision of the church, and they immediately knew that it was to help non-Christian people become obedient disciples of Jesus? It's not surprising that we don't achieve anything when most of us do not know what we're meant to be doing anyway.

Once you are clear on the main mission of the church, then you look at everything you do and see how it fits in. If it doesn't fit in, then you may have to say that it must go. It helps to streamline the activities of the church. Then, of course, other things may need to be added to help you get the job done.

Of course we are to worship the Lord. Of course we need teaching (primarily, it should be noted, on how to obey Jesus) and we need to do all the things that Jesus told us to do, but at the heart of it, the one thing that we want to be found doing when Jesus comes, is helping non-Christian people become obedient disciples of Jesus Christ.

'Helping to become' assumes a process. Everyone is somewhere on a journey. Our responsibility is to help them see where they are on that journey and enable them to move further along. The end process is discipleship. It is wonderful to know that Jesus has already promised us that those who seek will find. We now need to be led to those who are seeking.

In the account at the end of Mark's Gospel, it is recorded that Jesus said, 'Go into all the world and preach the good news to all creation. Whoever believes and is baptised will be saved...these signs will accompany those who believe....' He then lists all the wonderful miracles that would follow the preaching of the word.

After saying this, Jesus was taken up into heaven and we are told in verse 20, 'Then the disciples went out and preached everywhere, and the Lord worked with them and confirmed his word by the signs that accompanied it.' Here again is the command, and it's not a command to go; the assumption is that you've gone. 'Having gone, preach.' And the promise is that signs will follow the preaching.

I want to take a risk at this point and say that I think we may have got very distracted by our understanding of signs and wonders. Some have assumed that Jesus said, 'You do signs and wonders and people will come to Christ.' That's not what Jesus actually said here. He said that if we preach the gospel, then he would accompany it with signs and wonders. They would follow our obedience. The problem is that we have concentrated on signs and wonders and have assumed that if we can see a few miracles, the people will be saved. This puts everyone under great pressure because, in order to reach the lost, we must perform miracles. Jesus didn't say that. He said in effect, 'Go and preach the gospel. Tell them the good news, and following along behind will come signs and wonders, which God himself will do.'

I wonder whether there will be more signs and wonders and miracles when we start obeying Jesus. The majority of the miracles in the New Testament were among the unbelievers as a sign of the authenticity of what they were hearing. We have tried to have miracles among the saints, hoping a few non-Christians might spot them and be impressed. If we were to press on with sharing the gospel, and as a part of that offer to pray for those in need, we might be surprised at what would happen.

In Mark's Gospel, we are told of the response of those first disciples. They went out and preached the gospel everywhere. How they did it we are not so sure about, but that is certainly what they did.

Luke's Gospel is just the same. You don't quite get the same command, but Jesus said: 'Repentance and forgiveness of sins will be preached in his name to all nations... You are witnesses of these things' (Lk 24: 47-48). In other words, the gospel would go out and they were to be the ones to do it. Then, of course, in Acts 1 Luke continues the story, telling of Jesus' promise of the Holy Spirit to help them get the job done, and a reminder that they themselves would be witnesses to him.

I do not know how long we have before Jesus comes back, but the Holy Spirit seems to be stirring the church again and challenging us that the priority of our lives must change—not just as individuals, but as whole churches—to help non-Christian people become obedient disciples of Jesus.

If we know what the last thing was that Jesus told us to do, and we know he has not revoked that command, then the only question we must ask is: 'Are we doing it?' Even if we are not being very successful, the issue is whether or not we are at least seeking to obey. If not, then the question is: 'What are we going to do to change things?' For surely we must if we are to be obedient to him.

3
Removing the Blockages

I have found it helpful to try to analyse some of the reasons why we are making such incredibly slow progress at the moment. I do not believe we are to fall into an attitude of great guilt, but if there are areas where we have failed, we should acknowledge those and take steps to change. I realise that there are more than human factors involved. I know and believe we need an outpouring of the Holy Spirit and that ultimately nothing else will do, but that does not remove our human responsibility.

It is encouraging to look at other parts of the world where things have been happening, as this builds faith. But we need to bear in mind that there may well be many unknown factors at work in revival that we do not understand, therefore we must be careful not to slip into copy mode or fall back on technique. Having said that, it should encourage us to realise that what is possible in one part of the world might be possible here as well. We can learn from principles that others have learned, even though we must be careful not to assume that the transference of a technique will have the same effect here. An act of obedience in one situation may produce the desired effect there, but we are equally required to be obedient to God in our own situation. There may well be sociological factors that have made a country more fertile for revival than at another time in their history. Although we must believe for sovereign interventions of revival power, we have an ongoing responsibility to reach out, whatever the prevailing spiritual and sociological climate might be.

Many of the things I have listed here may appear negative, so please do not read this under a weight of condemnation! It is an attempt to realise where we are and to be honest with ourselves. Here are a number of factors that I have observed.

1. Spiritual oppression

There is no doubt that spiritual oppression exists in every city, town or area, and which makes it difficult for unbelievers to see and understand the gospel. It seems to be that there are times and places in which people are more open to the gospel than others. This is not the place to discuss territorial spirits, although the main question is not over their existence, but how to deal with them. I do not pretend to understand it entirely, but I do believe there is such a thing as spiritual oppression over an area, and the Bible intimates that the powers of darkness blind the minds of unbelievers. The only way to deal with that is through worship, prayer and strong proclamation of the gospel. If we understand anything of this battle, and most of us who have shared the gospel with others and found resistance are aware of the oppressive forces that cover people, then we must equally be aware that the only way through is to pray, praise and proclaim, and in time we will see a breakthrough. The difficulty with prayer is that the results are not immediately obvious to the eye and we easily become discouraged. The majority of us are carried along by the prayers of the few and we have limited the main burden of prayer to those we call intercessors, although it really is the job of the whole church. There will have to be a major change if we are to see the breakthrough we so badly need. We all know prayer is a key, but this knowledge does not seem to change the way we behave. We are trapped in our Western materialistic view, which seems to paralyse us from taking any real action.

Prayer of a united Church

I suspect we have a lot to learn about the effect of unity on prayer. It may well be that our prayer for towns and cities is greatly weakened because we are praying from a base that is impregnated by enemy strongholds due to disunity. When the church in a city or town begins to see itself as 'one church, many congregations' and repents of its divisions, it will remove the power base of the enemy within the church and therefore vastly increase its prayer effectiveness. We have a long way to go to understand fully the significance of this, but we fail to persue it at our peril. The very act of the church coming together will begin to see victories in the heavenly realm and cause release for the gospel to be preached and received. It is very easy to see unity as nice but not essential. We see it as something we will work at if we have the time, but the priority is getting on with the work in hand. We forget that the 'work in hand' is hindered by the oppressive atmosphere and that would be greatly changed by a church which closes ranks on the devil. The city in Nehemiah's day was a much stronger and safer place when the gaps in the walls were closed. We are trying to fight an enemy with gaping holes in the wall.

We also live in an environment of oppressive materialism. This is such a barrier to the gospel in the West. It would appear that in many countries where the gospel is running freely, there is a background of some sort of economic crisis. If this does not happen nationally, it may have to do so personally in order for there to be an openness to the gospel message in individual lives.

2. Tried and failed

The second thing that holds us back is that many of us feel we have already tried and failed. Most of us have, at some stage, attempted to share the gospel, or we've tried to bring somebody to Christ, and quite frankly we've not been very successful. Those people whom we've spent time with are still not Christians. We may have given up on it. When you fail in something, the natural thing is to try something else that has more obviously satisfying results.

Many churches have had a go at evangelism. They have spent a lot of time and effort in running a mission. It almost certainly cost a great deal of money. It promised so much and, in your honest moments, you have to confess that it produced very little fruit. It is tempting then to give it up as a bad job and concentrate on other things. So, if we feel that we are getting to be quite good at worship, or some other area in the church is flourishing, it's much easier to concentrate on that and put outreach on one side.

Just recently we were with some friends whose daughter was taking her first few strides in walking. She tried three times and each time she fell over. I didn't say, 'Don't press this. It's obviously not her thing. You could do a lot of damage to her. She could grow up really deeply discouraged because you pushed her into this. She might be very good at other things. We know she's good with her dolls and playing with bricks, so maybe that's her talent in life. She's good at eating and that sort of thing, so don't discourage her by making her do the thing that she obviously cannot do!'

What utter nonsense it would be if I had actually said that! We applauded her and told her to have another go. She might be walking across the room by now. But isn't that exactly what Jesus is always saying to us, 'I know you've tried and you've failed and you haven't got very far. Come on and have another go'? He told Peter after a hard night's failure in fishing to put down the net on the other side. He did so because he wanted to catch fish and because he had learned to obey Jesus. Peter's obedience was not conditional on being successful. It was enough to obey.

We must seek to make disciples. We must keep at it and one day we will feel the fresh wind of the Spirit blowing, and because we were out there seeking to obey, the nets will be stretched to the limits. It's at that point we will need everyone else to help. No wonder the Lord is also speaking to us all to build meaningful relationships of trust and commitment across the churches. He is wanting a net constructed that will be able to hold the enormity of the catch that is surely coming. The trouble is that when it is not happening, it is difficult to believe that it ever will. If there is one really effective weapon in the hand of the enemy, it is that of discouragement. In an age that is so success orientated, we are very vulnerable to it. If we do not think that we will succeed, we give up. No wonder Joshua was repeatedly told to take courage. He was going to know the opposite. Many of us have lost courage for lack of results. We must help one another to be full of courage and keep going.

3. Self-indulgence

Here's the third blockage – self-indulgence. The mention of this may make us feel very defensive, but there is a lot of truth in it—particularly for Spirit-filled, tongues-speaking, worship-released believers. We enjoy all of that so much, and so we should because God has given it to us. But what was given as a blessing can become an idol and a hindrance to the purposes of God. It is my observation that when we start to think more about reaching the lost and how we can change things to make them more effective, we quickly discover our areas of personal idolatry and selfishness.

It has been assumed, at times, that if we have really good and lively worship, non-Christians would come in and be thrilled with the sense of God with us in the place. They would realise what they had been missing all this time and want to come to Jesus. This is definitely true of some people, particularly those with a religious background. But in a highly-secularised society, for many people this is not necessarily the case at all. In fact, many will come to our high-powered meetings and conclude we are crazy. They are not used to singing, the words do not make any sense to normal people (I was at a service once where we all sang, 'Pierce my ear, Lord. Pierce my ear'!), they are made to stand for ages, there is no explanation of strange phenomena, and the sermon has nothing to do with ordinary life. Those of us who have been Christians for some time, completely forget what it is like to live in another environment and not know any of the religious language.

If we then decide we should alter our services because we are seriously wanting to invite unchurched people in, we will find a reaction: 'Don't take away my worship! Don't touch this; don't take away the other!' There's a terrible self-indulgence in us as Christians that puts our enjoyment and personal excitement ahead of anything else. Not that it isn't right to have good worship and praise; we don't want to lose that, but we can become incredibly self-indulgent. Somehow the church is there for 'me', to give to me, to help me, to keep me going, an oasis in my week. Is that what the church is really about? To provide an oasis for worn-out Christians? Surely it is also meant to be a power house to win the lost. Yet we have seen it solely as a place of refreshment, to help us survive another week.

Now it will do that. We will be refreshed, but let's not assume refreshment has to come from a particular liturgy, whether it be Anglican or charismatic new church.

Jesus said, 'My food is to do the will of him who sent me and to finish his work.' What was he doing at the time he said that? He'd just been talking to the woman at the well. 'That's my food,' he explained to them. 'Talking to this woman is my food. You've been down the road to McDonald's [that's the equivalent of where the disciples had been], but I'm full up. I've had a wonderful meal here talking to this woman. I have had such a fulfilling time!' Why? Because that was his food and drink. It is true. Seeing other people being touched by the Holy Spirit is much more satisfying than anything else we do.

I will say more about this later on, but it is a vital issue. We must discover how to help non-Christians enter into an experience with God, and not allow our self-enjoyment to get in the way. Some euphoric worship can be a wonderful experience of the presence of God, and some can also very easily be a demonstration of a desire for a nice feeling which is no more than overindulgent flesh. Either way, winning the lost may well require sacrifice on our part. Many families have used the motto 'FHB' at meal times with visitors. It stands for Family Hold Back, for the sake of those who are visitors. We may need to learn this lesson in other areas as well as food!

4. Disobedience

The fourth obstacle is disobedience. Some of us need to be honest here and admit that reaching lost people has not become a priority in our lives or the life of our church. When we find areas where we have not been obedient, we are not intended to be filled with condemnation, but we are meant to pick ourselves up and start again, rejoicing that God has shown us the way we should go. That is repentance.

Some people have the difficulty that their church building is pretty well full. Therefore, they assume that all is well. The main reason they are full may simply be that they are small and the Lord honoured their faith and filled the building up. The chances are that if they had a bigger place, he would fill that as well. If we want a real understanding of the true state of affairs, we must start to count the people outside the church, not just those inside. It's very easy to find reasons as to why we have not been reaching out, but the heart of the matter is that we have just been plain disobedient.

5. Wrong assumptions

The fifth blockage is that many people have wrong assumptions about evangelism. When the word 'evangelism' is mentioned, many of us assume we're talking about door-knocking, street preaching, thumping pulpits, grabbing people, or thrusting the gospel down people's throats. That's the sort of feeling it conjures up in many minds.

It has an aggressive feel about it. You hear people talk about 'doing evangelism'.

That is not what it is all about. It actually means expressing the love of Jesus through who you are to other people, in a way that they can find Jesus too. Somehow many people have backed off because they've thought that they cannot behave in that sort of aggressive way, and so assume that they can't become involved in evangelism. Of course, there is a place for the more overt forms of evangelism, but the vast majority of folk will share their faith in a different way from that.

Some people are evangelists by gifting, but the majority

are not natural evangelists in the sense of a ministry gift to the church. Nevertheless, Jesus gave this command to everyone and we have all been entrusted with the good news. Every Christian is to be involved at some point or other in the process of making disciples and helping people to obey Jesus.

I once decided to invent a word to describe the ministry of Jesus. Americans seem free to invent words, so I thought that I could. I used the word 'wasness'. My observation is that Jesus just was. I cannot imagine him dividing up his day and saying to the disciples, 'Well, today we'll have teaching until coffee time. After that we'll do some evangelism. After lunch, it will be healing and deliverance, and then tonight more evangelism.' He just was who he was. When a person came to him, he met their need, whatever it was. If we are going to reach a hurting world, we will need an army of ordinary people who, in their day-to-day lives, are always available. They will set out for work on Monday morning, saying to the Lord that they are open for business, whatever it is for that day. Then they are ready at any point in the day to meet the need of anyone Jesus brings to them. They will be looking out all the time for the opportunity to be his mouthpiece, his hands and feet. We need some more 'wasness' in our lives, by being Jesus' representative at every available moment.

The key to evangelism is the release of an army of ordinary people from Monday to Friday. Every working day in this country, hundreds of thousands of Christian people spend time with a vast number of ordinary unconverted folk. We do not need to have major campaigns to send people out to find the lost. We are falling over them every day of the week. Of course, if you see the same people day in and day out, there are limits to what you can do. But our greatest chance of changing the face of a nation is not just by crusades and missions, however good they may be, but by the empowering of a vast army of ordinary people who go off on Monday morning, full of the Holy Spirit, and ready for anything. Missions then become a time of reaping the fruit of the seed sown in the day-by-day sharing.

6. Lack of confidence

Then, sixthly, there's a lack of confidence. Personally, if you ask me to stand up and speak, I don't find it as hard as many. But when I get the chance to talk to my next-door neighbour about Jesus, I feel very nervous. I find it really hard, although I must say that it is incredibly rewarding when I do actually get to do it.

Most people do not find it easy. Isn't it encouraging to notice that the early disciples, who had been with Jesus and had experienced Pentecost and miracles, found it necessary to pray for boldness? If they needed to do so, how much more should we.

One of the main factors holding up the spreading of the gospel is that we are afraid. We may spend quite a bit of time praying for the lost. An even higher priority needs to be for us to have boldness. Most people have not yet heard the gospel, let alone rejected it. If they are going to hear, it will be from the lips of courageous believers. One of the main topics for every church prayer meeting should be the need for boldness. The answer is not to run away from the opportunities. The answer is to run to Jesus and say, 'I want more boldness. I need more confidence.' It would appear that one of the main features that singles out nations or areas experiencing great church growth as opposed to those that are not, is the presence or absence of boldness in the lives of the believers. This is easily as great a factor as the people who need to hear being open to the gospel. We easily hide behind the statement that people do not want to hear. The truth is that we do not know how people would respond if they heard, as most have never had the chance to hear. We cannot just pray for people from a distance and never give them the chance actually to hear for themselves.

7. Lack of contact

Seventhly, we encounter lack of contact. The sad truth is that the majority of Christians do not make friends with unbelievers. I'm in Christian work, so I do not get the contacts that most others do with unbelievers, therefore I'm in an even worse state. It is a challenge to us in our home at the moment that when we want to invite people round for a meal we will nearly always invite Christians. But we are having to reassess our lives to start inviting our neighbours and people we know who are non-Christians because that has to be the priority in our lives. Most of us don't have those contacts—we've got to build them. The better the fellowship, the less likely we are to have non-Christian friends. It is perfectly understandable that we will want to enjoy the company of our Christian friends, but that does not make it right. It could well be that the average non-Christian knows quite a few Christians, but they are unable to be really touched by the gospel because the Christians do not let them get close enough. There are many practical steps we could take, like inviting three or four folk for the evening—some Christians and the others not.

8. Fear

Eighthly, we must face up to the barrier of fear. Let's be absolutely honest about this. Fear stops us sharing our faith. We are afraid of looking foolish, afraid of rejection, afraid that we will not know what to say, afraid that our image will be spoiled, and afraid of a lot more besides. When Jesus sent out the disciples, he looked at them and said that they would be like a flock of sheep in the midst of wolves. For most of us that speaks of fear. It did not deter him from sending them out, but it did help them to know that he understood how they all felt.

It is quite natural to be nervous. Evangelism touches on most of our areas of insecurity. It highlights our own unsureness about the reality of faith. It makes us aware of our lack of knowledge, should we be pushed to answer questions. It shows us that the fear of man is very strong in most of us. It also makes us realise that deep down we are not sure that anyone else would really be interested.

The fear in us should help us to sort out a whole collection of other things. We need both to receive confidence and boldness from the Holy Spirit as well as to be as humanly prepared as we possibly can be.

The positive side of fear is that it helps us to treat people with respect. The over-confident person can come across as brash and rude, rather like a self-assured salesman. In fact, it is often quite effective to tell the person with whom you are trying to share your faith that you are feeling rather nervous about it all.

The opposite of fear, in this context, is faith. Isn't it interesting that so often when people talk about faith, and are heavily into 'faith', it seems to come down to money and miracles? We want faith for more money and faith to see miracles, but if my experience is anything to go by, I will tell you where we need more faith: it is faith to see the greatest miracle of all, that is, to see a person converted. Where I need faith is in the whole area of winning people for Christ. The other is comparatively easy. If you want to be in the big faith league, this is it!

If you want to be a man or woman of faith, then I would like to put out a challenge to you. I would address it particularly to the men, because, on the whole, men are far more reticent in the area of witnessing and sharing their faith than women. I've heard people, and particularly some younger people, say, 'There's no challenge in my life. What am I going to do with my life? I have a nice church, nice job, nice car. Where's the challenge in life?' You want a challenge? Jesus said, 'Make disciples.' Every one of us needs fresh challenges. I'd like to challenge you to make a disciple (help a non-Christian become an obedient disciple of Jesus) in the next six months. If you want a greater challenge, you won't find it anywhere.

So where do you start? Do you grab someone at work tomorrow and hound them to death? You start by talking to Jesus about it, since he knows where the seekers are. You ask, 'Who have you got in mind for me to help be an obedient disciple of Jesus?' He will show you. If you want bigger challenges to your faith, then believe for more, but they tend to come one at a time.

If we are going to see individuals released in sharing their faith in the work place, school, home or wherever, then the church itself needs to find ways to help to complete the job. In most churches, we have not provided what is needed. Many have excelled in their worship, praise and much of their teaching. But what happens is that many people who are not actually evangelists share their faith with friends at work, and they tell them about Jesus, but it doesn't go any further. Somehow they'd like to bring them to something on a regular basis so that over a period of time they can hear about Jesus, and decide for themselves, but there's nothing to which you can bring them. In most places, as far as I know, there's very little to take non-Christians to on a regular basis to hear the good news. I think non-Christians need two things:

1. They need a sense of safety. They need a place where they feel safe to come and where they're not going to be

embarrassed by what happens; where they will not be asked to stand up and introduce themselves; where they are made to feel that it's all right to join in as much or as little as they choose and that everything will be explained. They need to feel that they have not just gate-crashed a clique party, but that they are definitely wanted.

2. They need time. Many churches have guest services, but when we invite non-Christians to come and we share the gospel with them, they don't respond. The temptation is then to think 'Oh well, let's find somebody else. They're obviously not ripe fruit.' Or, they come and they are interested, but the next guest event is not for two months. That does not make it easy to consider Jesus at their own pace. It has been said that most men need to hear the gospel at least six times before they can make a decision. That is probably a very conservative figure. Most of us needed more time than that. I was talking to some folk from a church recently and they said that their experience was that for most people who aren't Christians, it would normally take six to eight months of hearing the gospel message weekly for them to become Christians. Most of us do not give people that amount of time and we wonder why so few are becoming Christians. Somehow we have to provide a place where they can come and be at home with us, share our lives, meet the Jesus whom we love and know, over a period of time. Few of us have done that up till now.

Another reason why people need time is that to really understand and to count the cost often takes time. Quick conversions can also be shallow conversions. We have often been guilty in the past, in our desire for results, of making it very easy to come to Jesus, and it has been afterwards that we discover it was only a spur-of-the-moment decision which did not mean much. Well-thought-out decisions are usually the deepest and most long-lasting. Jesus himself did not seem over-eager with some of the people whom he met. He wanted to be sure that they really had understood what it would mean to follow him. Having said that, we know that in some revival times, people are convicted very deeply, and very profound conversions can happen over only a brief period of time.

It should probably be mentioned here that unbelievers also need the opportunity to experience Jesus meeting their needs. A miracle in their lives (and it does not have to be a healing, as most people's felt need is not sickness) helps to open people up to the gospel. We need to help folk experience an answer to prayer in their lives, and this does not have to come in a high-intensity meeting, but through simply offering to pray for something tangible and practical.

9. Insensitive church

We did a survey once in the church, in which we asked the question: 'Would you bring your non-Christian friends to church?' The majority of people said 'no'. They loved the church, but they wouldn't bring people. So we asked: 'Why?'

Most people said things like, 'Because both they and we would be embarrassed. It's too unpredictable. Somebody might do something outrageous. The worship is too long.' Good, valid reasons.

I remember being asked to speak at an evangelistic service in one very lively church. I was really looking forward to it, as it was a great opportunity to preach the gospel. We stood up to sing the opening song and all the Christians started to dance round the hall. I thought, 'You can tell who hasn't brought any friends. You wouldn't do that if you'd brought your neighbours. Maybe you should, but you wouldn't. You'd be wondering what they thought about it.' So I worked out how many non-Christians were there, and there weren't many. If we are trying to win our friends to Jesus, we will behave slightly differently. Not because we want to hold back, but because we respect them. That's a valid reason. We don't want to kill the life and the joy, but we must start where they are.

We all have much to learn, and the chances are that we will not get it right all the time. But if we demonstrate the love of Jesus for a hurting world and do everything we can to reach out to them where they are and not demand that they are the ones who have to take a leap into our religious culture, we may yet love a lot of people into the kingdom.

10. Lack of understanding

Whenever we talk to someone who is not yet a Christian, we are never talking to someone who is totally objective in their thinking and in their consideration of what we are saying. If we do not understand something of the barriers many people have, we may misread their response. Most people are defensive and reactive when they first hear. If you were to take that as their final conclusion, you might miss completely what is really going on in their lives.

Let me list some of the main areas that are the cause of barriers people already have in their lives. Our job is to know which one is operating and to help the person come through the barrier.

(a) Prejudice

Everyone is prejudiced in some way. Many people from a religious background react strongly against the gospel. Their reaction is based on past hurt. They are only rejecting the religion of their memory.

Many have a fixed view of what a Christian is, so they respond according to their preconceived idea. They may be saying 'no', but it is not 'no' to the Jesus you are talking about, but the one they think of when you mention the name. It is always important to uncover what people's perceptions are before making assumptions based on their initial response.

(b) Pride

Most people are proud and are frightened of what others will think. There are very few men for example, for whom this is not a major problem in becoming a Christian. Often men will say they are not interested, but the truth is that they are afraid of the consequences.

(c) Fear

Fear of what it will cost is a major factor in people's thinking. They may be very interested, but fear will make them say things they do not really mean in order to keep you at bay.

(d) Intellectual reasons

Most intellectual questions are a smoke-screen to keep the gospel from getting too close, but there are always some genuine questions. If we care about people, we will make sure we know the answers, or at least know where they can be found.

(e) Moral issues

Here is the centre of the matter for most people, even if it is not expressed. When people realise that their particular lifestyle is being threatened, they won't admit to it, so they find another reason to keep themselves from having to take the gospel seriously. We need discernment from God to know what is really going on and to be able to help people through their difficulties and to help them admit things. Often, if they can see why they are reacting the way they are, then they can see the foolishness of their own behaviour and at least be honest with themselves.

(f) Ignorance

The average person who, in their mind, has rejected Christianity, has done so on a totally false premise. So when they say they don't want to be a Christian, they mean they do not want to go to church, or whatever else their concept of being a Christian is. It's quite good to know people's preconceived ideas, as it saves a lot of misunderstanding.

4
Motivation

> Now there were four men with leprosy at the entrance of the city gate. They said to each other, 'Why stay here until we die? If we say, 'We'll go into the city'—the famine is there, and we will die. And if we stay here, we will die. So let's go over to the camp of the Arameans and surrender. If they spare us, we live; if they kill us, then we die.' At dusk they got up and went to the camp of the Arameans. When they reached the edge of the camp, not a man was there, for the Lord had caused the Arameans to hear the sound of chariots and horses and a great army, so that they said to one another, 'Look, the king of Israel has hired the Hittite and Egyptian kings to attack us!' So they got up and fled in the dusk and abandoned their tents and their horses and donkeys. They left the camp as it was and ran for their lives. The men who had leprosy reached the edge of the camp and entered one of the tents. They ate and drank, and carried away silver, gold and clothes, and went off and hid them. They returned and entered another tent and took some things from it and hid them also.
>
> Then they said to each other, 'We're not doing right. This is a day of good news and we are keeping it to ourselves' (2 Kings 7:3-9).

'Are we doing right?' Shouldn't that be the key question for all of us? We have received so much and are now in danger of keeping it to ourselves. It's not deliberate, of course, as there is so much else to do, and anyway, we are so busy just keeping going with what we have. Examine the agenda for most of our church meetings and you will find that reaching lost people is a long way down the list—if it is there at all. Our programmes are so full. We can run a busy and apparently successful work without concerning ourselves too much that not many are becoming Christians. Growth has been so unbelievably slow in previous years that to see one person a week saved would be like a revival.

Does what I am saying make you a bit reactive and defensive? It does me! If so, it may not be a bad thing. We all need to face reality and examine ourselves on a regular basis. We are never meant to disappear under a cloud of guilt, but we should be honest with ourselves, and then look ahead and seek the Lord's direction for us.

It is always a very foolish thing to compare one church with another. A church in the suburbs, with students on tap, may look like a successful church. A smaller church in the inner city, surrounded by tower blocks and a multi-ethnic community, may appear to be struggling. How can you compare the two? The only conclusion you might come to is that the larger church should be putting resources like people and finances into the smaller church.

The call on our lives is to glorify God by helping non-Christian people become obedient disciples of Jesus. That is simply what God has told us to do. I recognise that when a person writes or speaks on this particular theme, it's very easy, particularly if you're a preacher, to induce guilt, fear and panic. You can produce a great sense of pressure. If you want to make anyone feel guilty in the Christian life, tell them that they don't pray enough, because they don't, and then talk about evangelism, because everybody says, 'I know we ought to, but...' and very easily pressure comes on.

The pressure comes because we so often build on wrong

expectations. Our understanding of evangelism is impaired by the stereotype image of going around aggressively grabbing people and behaving in a peculiar way.

I was in a town not long ago, and there was a dear man waving his Bible around and shouting at the top of his lungs in the name of Jesus. Nobody was listening and I felt incredibly embarrassed as I thought, 'Is this really what we're about? Am I with him or aren't I?' And I wasn't sure. And yet so much of our expectation of evangelism is like that—a sort of 'grab people and thrust something they don't want down their throat'. So whenever it's talked about we feel we don't want to associate with it and a fear and panic enters into us.

Often it raises painful memories of past experiences when we were made to do things we didn't want to do and we upset and embarrassed people. Somehow, we must take the sting out of that, because the call to evangelism is not to be based on guilt, but on obedience and love. It should create among us a corporate sense of expectation that people are going to become disciples of Jesus.

Let us look at a number of foundational issues.

Motivation

What is the motivation for evangelism? Recently, I overheard someone say, 'Oh no, we're pushing evangelism again.' I hope you do not respond like that, because the motivation is not to 'get evangelism done' just because that is something Christians and churches are meant to do. Let me give you some ideas of what I believe are the main reasons why we need to be sharing our faith with others.

1. Obedience to Jesus

In one sense, this is where it begins and ends. The nature of being a Christian is that we have decided, even if we struggle with it, that we will give our lives to obeying Jesus. The concept of being members of the kingdom of God means that Jesus is King. It is amazing how often we find ourselves debating issues which would be quickly solved by realising that we are simply called to obey. His word is never up for discussion; only obedience.

If we have problems with the whole issue of winning people for Christ and sharing our faith, we cannot complain. It is Jesus who told us to do it. In the same way that we are to forgive others, we're to love others, we're to give of our money, we are also to reach out in compassion and care for others. All the other things Jesus taught, we set out to do because we're Christians and the nature of being a Christian is that, in the power of the Holy Spirit, we seek to obey Jesus. That is what it means to live in the kingdom of God. We cannot be in that kingdom unless we intend to obey the King.

We choose to live sexually pure lives. We don't commit adultery. We don't sleep around, because Jesus taught us that it is the wrong way to live. Obeying Jesus because we love him is what it means to be a Christian. Jesus also said, 'Make disciples.' So it is part of our Christian life. We're to win people for Christ and bring them into the kingdom of God because Jesus told us to. If you're a Christian, it's part and parcel of being a Christian. If you say, 'We are now into evangelism,' it's like saying, 'We are now into obedience.' It is not an optional extra for the keen people. It is not open to debate or discussion. The question can never be, 'Should we be trying to reach the lost?' The only question is, 'How are we going to do it and how can we reach more?' We may all have different roles in the process, but we are all called to be involved somewhere along the line.

The fact that we all find it very hard should not deter us from putting it as a priority in our life together.

2. Love for Jesus

We love him. That is the heart of the Christian's testimony. When we begin to realise that Jesus died for every human being, and that on the cross he paid for every person's salvation, we can see why he has said to the church to go and collect; to go and bring in this harvest; to go and tell people the good news that the work is done. Jesus sacrificed his life for other people, and now he wants them to enjoy all that he has paid for on their behalf. Nothing more needs to be done for the salvation of every human being. The full price has been paid. It is now only a question of entering in. How will people know that they have been left a great inheritance unless someone tells them? The reason we must share good news with them is because Jesus wants to know them.

We do it for Jesus, because he wants to spend eternity with them, and it seems a tragedy that many of them are going to miss out on that. So we do it out of our love and our desire to please Jesus.

3. Sheer gratitude

Isn't that what those lepers found out? They were having a whale of a time taking and enjoying everything they could grab hold of, and suddenly they realised what they were doing. They had found something fantastic which they realised they shouldn't keep to themselves. We are to share our faith out of sheer gratitude.

I am thrilled to bits that I'm going to heaven. I'm so glad I know Jesus. I don't know what I would do if I didn't know Jesus, so I'm glad if I get the opportunity to tell other people about him. I don't find it easy, but it seems incredibly selfish not to want to tell others.

4. The reality of heaven and hell

It is from the lips of Jesus that we learn that when we die we either go to heaven or we go to hell. Surely we need to make sure that as many people as possible are going to heaven. There has been a lot of debate about the nature and duration of hell. Whatever the truth is, Jesus seemed to believe that hell was foul enough for him to die on the cross so that we can avoid it. Peter preached and urged the people to save themselves from the present generation, implying the judgement they were under. He had lived with Jesus for three years and no doubt was aware of Jesus' teaching on the subject. Most of us as Christians need to come to a fresh understanding of the reality of heaven and hell. Surely, if we truly believed, we would want so much for our friends to avoid hell and enjoy heaven. It's not a bad motivation. In fact, if we really believe these things, it is worth going to any ends to tell people. I don't believe we should set out to upset people, but if that is what it takes to shake someone into facing reality, it is worth it.

5. Love for people

Jesus was moved with compassion when he saw the people. When we look on the utter mess of people's lives, we know that only Jesus can help them. We know that the Holy Spirit can touch deep into the hearts of people to bring healing. We know that men and women who have suffered pain and rejection need to know the love of the Father. If we love people, then we will want to tell them about the Jesus who has done so much for us.

A process

To help non-Christians become obedient disciples of Jesus is a process. You might be involved with somebody anywhere along that process. Often we're a link in a chain. You might be someone who is always helping people to take that first step. You might be someone who gives a lot of time to discipling people who have just become Christians. It doesn't really matter, as long as between us we get people from where they are now to becoming obedient disciples of Jesus. We need each other to help in the process.

I was speaking at a meeting and a young man came up to me afterwards and said, 'Some time ago, when you came to speak at the university where I was studying, I came to all your meetings, but I didn't become a Christian. I left university a couple of years ago now and last month I became a Christian. When the time came I still remembered something of what you'd said.' I thought how good it was that the seed had been sown through those meetings and it was later he became a Christian. I had just a little part in his coming to Christ. Someone else had actually taken him through the last step. I believe that's true of all of us. We can sow seed somewhere along the pathway in someone's life.

It is a process in everyone's life. We need to help people along that journey.

It is said that any group of Christian people can be divided into two categories. Some are evangelists. It is usually reckoned that about ten per cent of any church have a gift of evangelism. That usually means they have the ability to bring people to the crisis point and lead them to faith in Christ. They are able to provoke something in people and cause them to respond. Usually, they are fairly outgoing in manner. Evangelists cannot help but tell people about Jesus. They can't understand why everybody else is so slow and holding back. It's a wonderful gift that they have from God and they must be encouraged to use it to the full.

The difficulty about this sort of talk is that it can easily cause the rest of us to sit back and say, 'Well, that lets me off the hook. I'm obviously not one of the ten per cent. I'll let them get on with it!' In fact, you may not be a natural evangelist, but you will unquestionably fall into the second category, because it includes every believer. Every one of us is a witness to what we have experienced. Whereas a barrister may have the skills to argue a case, everyone can be a witness to what they have seen, and everyone's life will bear witness to something or other.

You are a witness to the love and power of Jesus. If something has happened in your life, then you are a witness to this great thing that has happened. We express this in different ways.

First, in being. That is, just by being a Christian. You say, 'I didn't witness to anybody last week'. Yes you did, unless you stayed in bed all week. When you were out at work, when you were out shopping, when you were on the bus, you were a witness. You say, 'I never talked about Jesus once.' Maybe not, but you were a witness. The Spirit of God in you was showing something to other people. There are people all around you at work who know you are a Christian. You've never opened your mouth, but I expect they know. They may think you are weird, but there's something about you that is different. You are a witness because the Holy Spirit is in you. That's why it is important for us to touch as many lives as we possibly can.

There's a lovely scripture in John 1 that speaks of Jesus: 'The Word became flesh and dwelt among us.' The word 'dwelt' actually has the sense of pitching a tent. It says of Jesus that he became flesh as a human being and he 'pitched his tent' among us. Some of us have been camping and we know only too well what happens when we pitch our tent. One of the things we discover, and most people forget this, is that canvas is not as thick as brick. The consequences can be very funny. It's extraordinary how, after people go into their tents at night, you can hear the most amazing conversations if you are really quiet.

You can't camp on a campsite and expect to be totally private. You affect everybody around you.

Jesus, as it were, 'pitched his tent' on earth so that everybody could touch his life. That is what he is calling us to do. That is why it is important for us to spend time with people who are not Christians; invite them for a meal; join the clubs around us; go to things with people who are not Christians; spend time with them, and that means not just at work. In just being with people something will rub off, even before you say anything. You must trust the Holy Spirit in you to do the work. He is more eager to touch other people than you and I are. We must at least help by getting as close to them as possible.

It is easy to think after a hard day's work, 'I'm glad to get out of here. At least I've got home group tonight where I can mix with my Christian friends.' That's great, and that is what the group is for, to strengthen and encourage us. But we need to spend time with those who are not Christians. Not to preach at them, but to be who we are with them. It won't take long before they ask us some questions. Something will cause the conversation to turn in such a way that we can share something of our faith.

We must learn to encourage one another as much as we can, to give plenty of time to being with people who aren't yet Christians, so that we can express in our life something of the love of Jesus.

In 2 Corinthians we are told that we are the aroma of Christ. People sniff us. We are a fragrant aroma to those people who are looking for life. As we walk into our office or other place of work, there's a sense of fragrance because Jesus is with us. But, even though that is true, it is only part of the story, as we will need to be able to speak as well. We will need to be able to verbalise our faith and, let's face it, that's the hard part, because we so easily become tongue-tied. We treat opportunities with a mixed response: half-glad that they've been provided, but half-wishing they hadn't because we are not sure what to say that won't sound corny. There is no harm in having prepared roughly what we might say if we are put on the spot.

At the end of the day, though, it comes down again to motivation. This is far more important even than using a good method or having a pat message. The motivation is that we love Jesus. The motivation is that we're committed to him to be obedient to him. The motivation is that people are going to hell. The motivation is that we are extremely grateful.

If I saw a building on fire and someone said to me as I walked past, 'Go in there and tell the people the building's on fire and get them out as soon as possible,' I could say, 'OK. What do you suggest I say? Shall I go in there and say, "The building's on fire," or should I say, "Don't panic, anybody," or should I say...?'

'Go and tell them!' they would reply in desperation.

'Well, I've never done this before. What should I say? How would you best express it? Do you think one sentence or several? What should be my introduction?'

'Get in and tell them the building is burning.'

So I would say, 'OK,' and I would run down the street, into the hall, and I would shout to all the people, 'Get out! This place is burning down.' And they would rush outside and see the place on fire before it crumbled to the ground.

Later, as we're standing outside, someone might come up to me, panting away, and say, 'I'll just take you on one side, if you don't mind. It was you who told us, wasn't it?'

'Yes, it was me.'

'I just wanted to say that you've obviously never done that before. There's a very good book out on how to do it. Also, I'll get you a tape on how to tell people about burning buildings. You'd find a more gentle approach is much more satisfactory.'

Somehow, I don't think he'd do that. I think he'd come up, hug me and say, 'Thank you for telling us.'

When I became a Christian, the guy who led me to the Lord had never read any of the books, so he really hadn't got a clue about the finer details of evangelism. The first thing he said to me one day was 'Nick, have you ever asked Jesus into your life?' This was between a maths and a physics lesson. I thought he'd gone completely nuts. I didn't know any of this jargon at all. The next day he asked me almost the same question, except he said, 'Have you asked Jesus into your life yet?' I was so angry with him. I thought I *was* a Christian, and I didn't understand what he was talking about. So we had a long argument and we argued late into the night on many occasions. He got to me. Not long after that I became a Christian. I had known above everything else that he was sincere and that he was real. I had known him for a long time and I had seen the change in his life, although I was unsure what had caused it. So the words he spoke were secondary to the way in which he said them.

I was so grateful to him because he had introduced me to Jesus. I didn't say 'Charles, I think you need to read some books! There's some good books on evangelism you need to read, because you're not very good at it.' I was just grateful that he had such a strong motivation. It excited him so much to become a Christian that he wanted to tell me.

Enthusiasm, of course, should not take the place of having thought out the best way to say something, but motivation must be there if we are going to get the job done. It is better to communicate badly but with enthusiasm than not at all.

5
Reaching out in Style

Not only do we need to examine our motivation, but also our whole attitude to life. If we understand the gospel at all, then we will feel that it is an incredibly important thing for people to find Christ. Presumably, we all try to do our job to the best of our ability. If you're a doctor, you try to do your doctoring well, and you try to be good to your patients. If you're a mechanic, you try to be a good mechanic. If you're a bus driver, you try to drive the bus well and considerately and be nice to the passengers. I imagine most of us try to live out our lives as Christians in the area of our calling the best we possibly can.

But is that all? Is that good enough for us? Surely there should be something in all of us that burns inside and says, 'What I really want in my life as I touch people day by day, is to see them find Jesus in the way that I have. I may not know how and I may not be very good at communication, but I want to use my life to win people for Christ, even if I am only part of a process in their lives. I may be the first step on the way, or perhaps the last part of the way, but I want to be intervening in the lives of ordinary people so that they too can find Christ.'

Is that deep in your heart? I believe it needs to be in all of us because it is the desire of the Holy Spirit. It will be more strongly in the evangelists, but it will be there in every person who is a Christian, even though many of us will have suppressed it in the pursuit of other things. Do you see your medicine, your bus driving, your mechanic's job, your secretarial work as some way of touching the lives of other people?

When a friend came back from holiday, I asked him if he'd had a good time. He said, 'It's been fantastic.' I asked him what had been the highlight and he said, 'I talked to two people about Jesus.' He was excited because he saw something happen. By nature, he is not an outgoing person and would not find talking about his faith easy. He had been available and the Lord had opened up the opportunity for him.

Then we need to ask the question, 'What style do we use and feel most comfortable with?'

It is important to understand that people who aren't Christians are open to hear the gospel in different ways, depending on their personality and their background. In the same way we are all different and we all tend to prefer different ways of sharing our faith. We just need to trust God to connect the right person with the right person!

Some people can only hear it one way—when it's shouted at them. Some people react against that and they will only hear when it is communicated in a gentle way. Every person who isn't yet a Christian needs to hear the good news in a way that suits them and in such a way that they will be able to hear. All of us became Christians in a different way and through different means.

The good news is that we are all different and our means of communication are different. It is a shame when we think there is only one way and deny what God has made us.

We share the gospel, the good news of Jesus, according to our own personality, because that's how God made us. He's not asked you to be like me. He's not asked me to be like somebody else. He's asked you to be you and me to be me. There may be times, as Paul found, when we need to adapt to the situation we find ourselves in, but normally it will be in the context of what we find natural. The love of Jesus just flows through us as we are. He will use our personality, and the world needs to hear the gospel through different personalities so people can hear the good news in a way they can understand. It's such a shame that we have somehow assumed that to share our faith in Christ with people needs one particular method. It doesn't. There must be variety. It means expressing the love of God through who we are. The message is the same, but the messengers are different.

Don't let the fear you may feel confuse you by telling you, 'You've got the wrong approach because you are still afraid. If you were using the right method, you would not be afraid.' You need to know that any form of sharing your faith may have an element of fear because it needs faith. You need to find the way you feel most comfortable with. But make sure you use that way to say, 'I want to reach out through my particular personality to help others find Jesus.'

Recently, in the church of which I am a part, I played everyone a tape of the well-known song 'There is a Redeemer'. I then played the same song (recorded for me by a friend) in a Country and Western style. Some with good taste loved it! Others didn't. Then we had it in Reggae; then in a very up-tempo rock style, which was not everyone's cup of tea. It was the same song, same lyrics, but different styles. It appealed to different people as it was played in different styles.

In exactly the same way, we must be free to share our faith in different ways according to who we are. People will hear the truth when it is presented in such a way that they can understand. That will vary enormously from person to person. Different people warm to different styles.

Some of us will only hear a message through a rock style. Some of us will only hear it through a Country and Western style. Differing musical styles here are a picture of differing lifestyles. We're all different. The message, the song, the words, the lyrics were identical on all four tapes but some of us preferred one thing to another. So it is in our evangelism; in our reaching out and sharing Jesus with others.

Therefore, we must be free to present Jesus in many ways and not be stereotyped. Let the Holy Spirit flow out through who you are. That is the way God has made you to be, so be yourself and let him work through you.

To give some ideas about different approaches, I've listed some below. I am grateful to Bill Hybels for the headings in his book, *Honest to God*. I found them very helpful and have used them here, and added some personal comments. What you will notice is that most of us use a variety of approaches, but feel most comfortable with one or two.

1. Confrontational approach

All of us know people who are confrontational in their approach. It would appear that Peter was. 'What must we do?' they asked after he had preached. 'Repent!' was his straight reply, and he followed it up by warning them to 'save themselves from this corrupt generation.' Strong words! Peter was very straight and up front. His mouth was quick on the uptake, with no beating about the bush. He was a confrontational person.

Some of us are like that and find it natural to challenge people with such words as, 'Are you saved? Do you know Jesus? Why not?' That may be your approach and you feel easy in it, but it's not everybody's style. It's an aggressive and confrontational style which some need if they are going to respond, but it may also frighten some people silly.

I remember doing a mission years ago and a vicar from the North of England was on the team. He was very confrontational. One day we were standing on the pavement next to a parked car. He banged on the window. The driver wound it down and said, 'What do you want?'

He said, 'You are a lucky man.'

The driver replied, rather startled, 'Why?'

My friend said, 'Look at your registration plate.' (It included the letters GLM.)

The driver said, 'So what?'

'It says GLM. Don't you know that stands for God Loves Me? Every day you look at your registration plate it tells you God loves you. You are a lucky man.'

The guy wound up his window and drove off. I bet he's never forgotten the incident!

I was in a shop in Birmingham with a friend and there was music on. We were trying to talk to the sales assistant, who apologised for the loudness of the music. The person I was with said 'Isn't this just like life? There are so many things going on around us that we can't hear the real message. Do you know the real message is that God loves you and Jesus has a purpose for your life?' I was thinking, 'We only came in here to buy a shirt.' But it seemed easy when he did it.

When Arthur Blessit was here we knew we would never leave a restaurant until at least one person had heard about Jesus. He did it in a very nice way, but it was pretty confrontational.

You say, 'That's not my style.' But it is for some people. If it is, go with it because there are many people who need that.

I remember going to a meeting and after I'd spoken, people were leaving to go home. As they did so, I said 'goodnight' to one man, and asked him if he was a Christian. He said he wasn't, so I asked him why not. He said, 'I don't know.' I asked him why he hadn't become a Christian and he said, 'Because nobody ever asked me.' I asked him if he wanted to become a Christian and he said he did. We went and prayed together.

Some people need to be confronted.

2. Apologetic and discussion approach

This style is one that is more into discussion. I know people who have non-Christians round to their homes and have discussions, and they talk and share about the apologetics of the faith: why we can believe in God; why it's reasonable to believe the Bible, and that sort of thing. If you're the kind of person who walks around with a Bible in one hand and Josh McDowell's books in the other, because that's the way you feel most comfortable approaching things, then go with it because there are lots of people who like to think things through. There are many good books around that you can give to people and then arrange to see them again and discuss what they have read. I remember we used to use a booklet with students called, *Christianity for the open minded*. We would say to a student, 'Are you open minded?' It was rare for people to say they weren't, so we gave them the booklet to read and then met up with them later.

It is a very good principle always to have a book or booklet handy, as you never know when you may need it. In fact, a selection of different ones is helpful, as different people are asking different questions.

Most of us have a number of approaches operating at different times, and this is certainly a common one.

3. Testimony approach

This is incredibly important and it is good for everyone to be ready to use it when the opportunity presents itself. They say that the person with an experience will always win over the person with an argument. The purpose of testimony is just to be able to say, 'This is what happened to me.' It's like the blind man in John 9. He was healed and the Pharisees came up to him and asked him how he received his sight.

He replied, 'He put mud on my eyes, and I washed, and now I see!'

So they beetled off to his parents. 'How is it that he can now see?'

That's the testimony approach and it is used at times when you're with people and are not quite sure what to say, so you share from your own experience of what has happened to you and how Jesus changed your life.

'I gave my life to Jesus, and he's changed my life.' Or, 'In this situation I find I can pray and Jesus really helps me.' This is just simple testimony about what God has done.

Often it is such a simple thing for all of us to do. We can feel rather tongue-tied, so it is not a bad thing if we can work out ahead of time roughly what to say. Since we never quite know when the opportunity will come along, it is good to have rehearsed something so that we will speak clearly and be a help to the person concerned.

4. Relationship approach

This again is key for most people. It involves spending a lot of time with people, having them in for meals or coffee, and sharing in order to develop relationship. Some may develop into real friendship and some may not. Most people, or so it would seem, become Christians out of relationships. It is usually through friends that people are introduced to Jesus. If we are going to see people come into the family, the likelihood is that it will be through this means. Some people have suggested that this is a rather poor reason to begin a friendship. Actually, it is a very good reason. Can there be a better motivation than wanting the very best for someone? And the best is to be saved from hell and to get to know Jesus. Having said that, most of us start friendships because we want to get to know people, and we are not doing it with the proviso built in that they must become Christians, and if they do not we will break off the friendship! Friendship gives people the opportunity to observe Christianity first hand and see it applied through ordinary lives.

In the gospel story, Matthew is an interesting case in point. As soon as he met Jesus and became a disciple, he wanted to introduce his friends to Jesus. So he did the thing that would make him and his friends feel most comfortable; he held a party. That was something he knew how to do well. He liked to build relationships and he already had lots of friends, so through his friendships he was able to share Jesus. He did not go and preach on their doorsteps or put pressure on them, he just exposed them to Jesus and waited to see what would happen. If we have people in our home regularly and let them touch our lives, we expose them to Jesus and something will happen.

5. Invitational approach

There are many, many people who find it quite difficult to express themselves very well, and are embarrassed to talk openly about Jesus, and so the easiest thing for them to do is invite them to come and hear those who can. To invite someone to a meeting is often the best thing to do.

The woman whom Jesus met at the well, as recorded in

John 4, is a good example of this. She had a conversation with Jesus and as soon as she realised who Jesus was, she dashed off into town. She stood up in the town and said, 'Come on, everybody and hear this man. He's told me everything I ever did.' She didn't actually tell them about the gospel, the good news, but she invited them to come and meet the man who would tell them everything.

The difficulty that so many face is that if there isn't a Billy Graham crusade on, there is very little around that we feel confident to bring someone to. This is something that has got to change and may be a good reason to re-examine our church services or lay on some regular alternative for people to bring their friends to.

My own experience is that although we will major in one approach, we may find we use different ones at different times. I think for the majority of Christians it is much easier to invite somebody to hear someone speak and explain the gospel, or invite them to an event, than it is to say straight out, 'I want to tell you about Jesus.' I remember years ago when I was a student in London there were regular meetings every month in a hotel, and we were able to take friends along. I found it very easy to invite people to this—especially as it was not in a religious context. That's one of the reasons why we want to provide safe places in which to hear a dangerous message, so that it is as easy as possible to say to a friend at work, 'Come along.' You may feel embarrassed to say, 'I want to tell you about Jesus,' but you may find it quite easy to say, 'I'd like to introduce you to my church. Come along one day. It's a bit different. I think you'll like it. Come, and bring the family.'

6. Serving approach

In Acts 9, we read of a wonderful lady called Tabitha (or Dorcas as she was renamed), whom Jesus raised from the dead through Peter's prayer. She was a woman who used to sew and make things for people. She served the community. In her serving she was able to lead people to Jesus. Some folk are like that. They find that's the way they can best get alongside people. These people reach out to their neighbours by doing things for them. They help them in different practical ways and through that people see the love of Jesus.

So, the various approaches to telling people about Jesus include confrontation, apologetics, testimony, relationships, invitations and serving, and there is a multitude of other ways. Each way expresses who we are to other people.

Meeting the felt need

We usually find ourselves wanting to tell people that they need to come to Jesus and be forgiven. We see that as their primary need and so we face them with it. Most people see their needs differently. Their felt needs are rarely for salvation, but for some very practical day-to-day thing. Jesus had a way of meeting people's felt needs and this led on to salvation. I believe God loves to answer the prayers of seekers. He is longing to help them see that he loves them and cares about every area of their lives. Very often the best way to introduce someone to Jesus is to ask if you can pray for a need. When Jesus answers that need, they are then interested to find out more. Our fear is that the prayer will not be answered. How weak is our faith in a loving God! In some places prayer cells have been set up in streets and they have offered to pray for the needs of people in the street. There have been some very exciting results.

Why should this not be a routine approach for every Christian at work or wherever they are? As soon as you hear of a practical need in a person's life, offer to pray. Then come back to them to find out what has happened. I do believe this is a vital missing key in our evangelism today. We must introduce men and women to the living Jesus who wants to meet them where they are.

It is being supernaturally natural, and naturally supernatural in order to bring the good news about Jesus to other people. Somehow we must take the sting out of all the false expectation in evangelism, but put in the challenge and encourage adventures in faith by saying to one another, 'Let's go out into our week and be ourselves, filled with the Holy Spirit. I want God to provide me with the opportunity to be able in some way or other to help a person from being a non-Christian to become an obedient disciple of Jesus. I want to help someone along that road to faith this week. I want to be doing something with my life that is infinitely worthwhile.' Somewhere we'll be the link in the chain. Every one of us can get involved with someone, somewhere, and be influential in somebody's life. And we can do this without losing our integrity and turning into some kind of machine or stereotype of what we have thought evangelism to be. We need to touch other people's lives long enough so that the good news can get out.

6

Near, Now and Natural

One of the difficulties of speaking or writing is that you say what you think are the right words, but people don't actually hear the words you're saying. A guy went into an ironmonger's shop and said, 'I'd like to buy some nails.'

The shopkeeper said, 'How long do you want them.'

The guy replied, 'Don't be silly, I want to keep them!'

You may have heard of the notice in an upstairs restaurant which read, 'If you don't want a full meal, why don't you try our coffee and roll downstairs?'

Downstairs there was another notice which said, 'If you think our waitresses are rude, then you should see the manageress!'

We can often say things in life and use the right words, but they have a number of different meanings and people see them in different ways. It's certainly true of the word 'evangelism'. It means different things to different people and certainly brings up different images in our minds, depending on our experience.

I believe God has been giving the church a renewed heart and desire to reach the lost. We are just beginning to realise how far we have come from it and how large the gap is that has to be overcome. A few enthusiastic sermons, calling the church to battle, will not do it. It is going to take a determined and calculated effort to redirect and focus the church. It will require a major change of heart in most of us. It is only as we begin to do this that we become aware of how far we have come and how much we resist change.

Earlier, I wrote about the last thing Jesus told us to do. It's not a question of whether I want to be into evangelism or not, it's a question of obedience. If we love Jesus and want to be obedient to him we will do the last thing he told us to do. This is the call to the whole church as the different gifts work together and as we live out our lives in the world. Jesus said that we are both salt and light and he urged the first disciples not only to be careful of losing the saltiness, but also of hiding their light. If we are the only source of real light in our world, what a disaster it would be if that light were hidden away.

The prime motive for this is not because we want people to join our church so that it can become bigger, although church growth is an inevitable result of winning the lost. But it is that we want men and women to have a full life. It is not even so that we can start more churches, although that would be wonderful. It is because we want people to have the best possible life. We have discovered that this is a life lived with Jesus in obedience to him and so we must want to help others to discover this as well.

We are called to proclaim the message of Jesus both through means that are familiar and those that are less familiar. The most common and the most natural will be through what is most familiar to us and that means sharing our faith while going about our normal routines of life. I referred earlier to the story told in John 4 about how Jesus met the woman at the well. There we are told of how the disciples went off to get lunch, and while they were gone, Jesus had a conversation with the woman which led to her telling the whole village about the amazing discovery she had made. When the disciples returned, Jesus said to them:

> Do you not say, 'Four months more and then the harvest'. I tell you, open your eyes and look at the fields! They are ripe for harvest. Even now the reaper draws his wages, even now he harvests the crop for eternal life, so that the sower and the reaper may be glad together. Thus the saying 'One sows and another reaps' (vv 35-37).

Here in this familiar story, Jesus teaches us a number of things that are vital in understanding evangelism.

He tells the disciples: 'Open your eyes and look at the fields!' If ever there was an appropriate text for us today, surely this is it. This is not a command to casually glance around. It is a command to alter our gaze and to fix our eyes on something...the harvest around us. For many of us it will require a clear change in the way we are looking. Here are three other important things we can learn from this passage.

1. Near

First, this incident reminds us that most people we are to share the good news with are very near. It was as if he were saying to the disciples, 'You think you've got to go far away to share the good news, but actually, the person who needs to hear the good news is right in front of your nose and you've not seen them. It's the person right near you.' They had not even considered that the Samaritan woman was a candidate to hear the gospel. It was as if she did not even exist. Jesus was not blinded by prejudice but immediately saw a woman in need. At the moment when the disciples were concerned about their lunch, Jesus spotted a woman in need.

I believe God is reminding us all that before we feel we have to go to the furthest corners of the earth, there are people right on our doorstep, right where we work, right in our neighbourhood, right in our school, right in front of our nose. They are the people with whom God has already brought us into contact. They are the people to whom we are already a witness. The people we are to share the good news with are very near to us. We don't need to look very far. Through familiarity or prejudice, we may be missing the very people God has in mind for us to speak to. Nearness does not necessarily refer to the geography of where we live. It has more to do with relationships. Most people do not have their closest relationships in the place where they live. It has more to do with the circle of people they spend time with, either at work or in some leisure activity.

2. Now

Secondly, I believe it reminds us that for many people the good news needs to be heard now. It is as if he is saying that we are always putting it off by convincing ourselves, 'It's up ahead. It's three months away. We're going to have a mission in a few years. We're going to plan to do some evangelism. We're going to go out.' It is so much easier to be planning something up ahead so that we do not have to do anything now.

The alarming fact is that very often missions have an overall negative effect on evangelism. It is not that holding a mission is wrong in itself, but it is the way in which it is done. When it is decided to hold a mission a year or two away, it means that very little outreach is done for that period, and it may actually stop. The process is usually that there is a period of training in evangelism which is often, if not always, unrelated to ordinary life situations. Then there is the mission itself in which people are invited to meetings and are often aware that the only reason they are being invited is because of this special mission that is on. Then afterwards, everyone is exhausted and there is the feeling that the mission has now been done, and there is a cessation of evangelism. This, in spite of the fact that a number of people may now be closer to the kingdom than they were before and are left high and dry. This scenario is not always the case, but it does happen a great deal. Continuous evangelism with special mission periods is a much better approach.

Jesus was saying to those first disciples as he says to us today, 'Now is the time, because there are people who are ready to hear the good news now, today.' And incidentally, some of those who are ready today may be dead if we leave it too long.

3. Natural

Thirdly, it is natural. It is near, it is now and it is natural. This was an easy conversation that Jesus had. He did not stuff a tract down this woman's throat. He was not obnoxious to her. He didn't grab her by the lapels and say, 'Are you saved?' He had a conversation with her about a drink of water and out of that he shared with her something of the love of God the Father. And as we know, her life was changed. It was a natural, easy thing to do. It may well be that the first port of call for most of us as Christians in sharing our faith, are those people who are near us. It should be done in as natural and easy a way as possible before we ever do something that is more aggressive, and before we consider a more penetrating approach into cultures that we have not reached, or groups that we've not yet contacted.

Who are the people we are going to reach? Let me list three groups of people.

First, there are the friends and acquaintances of members of the church. Remember Jesus said to go out to Jerusalem, Judea, Samaria and to the uttermost parts of the earth. Start where you are. People who are most readily available to us to share the good news with are our friends and our acquaintances, the people we work with.

Secondly, it's an interesting exercise to survey the church and to see the age group and backgrounds of the people who come. If these are the people you are at present attracting, then it is probably best to go for more of the same, because that is obviously who you are most effective in reaching. For example, you might find that the average age is thirty-five. In other words, thirty to forty is the main grouping of people you've been attracting to your church. That will be the main age group who are most open to hear the good news of Jesus through you. Not that you shouldn't talk to elderly people, but the people who are going to be most open in your context will probably be those from twenty-five to forty-five. If you decide to target the people who are not there in order to achieve a more balanced age group, you may well fail unless you have a clear strategy as to how to do so. It is much better to play on your strengths than work on the weaknesses. If you do what you do well, other churches will almost certainly fill the gaps.

At the same time, it is worth noting that statistics indicate that in the Western world, a very high percentage of people who become Christians do so before they reach the age of twenty-one. What does that say about the youth work in the church? It certainly does indicate which is the most open generation. Surely we should go to the harvest field that is ripest and expect that people will respond. In other words, if you have the capacity to do so and you want to touch the most open people, then the younger generation are the best to target. That will almost certainly mean giving money and resources into that area.

Thirdly, I believe we need to share the gospel with men as well as women. That sounds rather obvious, but I think it is fair to say that women on the whole tend to be much freer in sharing their faith with others. It would seem that generally speaking, women are less embarrassed about sharing their faith than men, and also women are more open to the gospel. Men need to be confronted. Most men need at some point in their lives to be eyeballed and asked, 'When are you going to do something about it?' I think it is important we should state that we are looking to win men for Christ. This is not to say we're not trying to win women and whole families for Jesus, but I believe the men in the church, vast numbers of whom have opted out and taken the easy and comfortable option, have a responsibility to win the men for Jesus and to make that their prime goal.

7

Steps in the Right Direction

Here are some steps that we should consider, both individually and as a church, if we are going to take seriously the challenge of achieving this goal.

1. Make a decision

We must make a decision in our lives, both personally and in the corporate life and vision of the church, to make non-Christian people a priority in terms of time and energy, because they matter to God. That means a decision has to be made. It will not happen by chance. It will probably not happen if you wait until everyone feels like it. There will always be easier things to do and good reasons why it should be put off. It is a decision that leaders must make if the church is to be relevant to the world we live in.

There's a fascinating story in Luke 15 in which Jesus, in essence, says: 'Imagine a shepherd who has 100 sheep, and one of them is lost. What will the shepherd do?' The natural answer to that question is that he will stay with the ninety-nine because at least those are safe and he must be careful not to lose any more. But Jesus says, 'The shepherd will go after the one that is lost because his heart is for the lost.' That parable tells us something about the heart of God.

If Jesus were here in the flesh and he was walking down

my road with his disciples saying, 'I need to go somewhere for lunch,' I wonder where I would suggest he went. If he then asked my opinion, I would naturally want him to come and visit us. I can't think of anything more incredible in the whole wide world than to have Jesus in my home for lunch. As I have thought about this, it has made me realise how easy it is to want to keep Jesus to ourselves. Having thought about it for a time, I concluded that in fact I'd line up some of my neighbours and say to Jesus, 'I'd like you to go there for lunch.' Then, afterwards, I'd like to go and find out what happened! Although that won't happen today, we can all bring Jesus into other people's lives by taking him through our lives to those who do not know him.

When Jesus talked about the lost sheep, he was in a house, sharing with a group of sinners. He was mixing with the tax gatherers, the sinners, the backsliders. He wasn't with the religious people. Why? Because his attitude was, 'You think you are fine. I'm going for the people who are lost.' Therefore, this must be the priority in our lives as his present-day disciples. We have eternity to spend with each other. Not that we should neglect one another. Of course we are to have fellowship together with other believers, as that is how we encourage and strengthen each other. It should be noted that fellowship in the New Testament does not describe drinking coffee together. It is referring to a participation in a common task. Our greatest fellowship is actually fellowship in the gospel. Our common desire to share the gospel unites us together in fellowship. Going through hardship or a common experience is the best way for people to find deep relationship with one another. One of the reasons that so much of our Christian fellowship is so weak is that we are not working together for common goals, but trying to relate while doing and achieving very little.

Our priority at this time must be to spend time with unbelievers because we want them to be touched by the good news of Jesus. This is so much easier to write about than to do. It is our natural inclination to want to spend quality time with our Christian friends. After all, it is with them that we have so much in common, and they are the ones with whom we can easily relate. The better the sense of community in the church, the more difficult it becomes to break out of the ghetto mentality.

We have to make that decision, because Jesus loves lost people.

I remember some years ago driving down the M1 in someone else's car, and it broke down. It seemed a very long time before the AA arrived. Eventually they came and I hoped it would not be anything serious.

I said to the mechanic, 'Is it serious?' and he said, 'Yes!'

He towed the car off to the garage, which was in the middle of nowhere. I asked the man in the garage if it would take a long time, and he replied that I'd have to leave it and come back another time. That meant I had to take the bus and train home. I asked him for the nearest bus stop and he pointed me to a place where the buses went every hour.

I said, 'Lord, I pray there's one about to come,' because I was late and needed to get home. I got to the bus stop and I discovered one had gone five minutes before. I thought, 'This is not my day.'

So I wondered what I should do for the remaining fifty-five minutes, and decided to hitch a lift, which I hadn't done since I was a student. A little green mini stopped within two minutes. I jumped in, and the first thing the driver, a young business type, asked me was what I did for a living. I said I was in full-time Christian work, and he replied, 'Oh, fantastic!' which wasn't what I was expecting. I asked him what he did and he told me. Then this is almost word for word what he said to me: 'For many months now I have been thinking about Christianity and I have been praying to God to find me someone who will explain to me what it means to be a Christian'. I sat in the car thinking, 'Goodness me! Did God plan this all along?' And for half an hour, between there and Leicester, I was able to tell him what it meant to be a Christian and how to become one.

It was difficult after that to complain about the car breaking down and the resulting frustrations, because I recognised that God loves lost people. I do not know if he went to all those lengths in order for me to talk to the man, but I wouldn't blame God if he did. Somehow he needed to find somebody who could explain to this young man that Jesus loved him. He loved him so much that he wanted him to hear. Jesus has already told us that anyone who is seeking will find. Our job is to be available every day and anywhere so that God can lead us to seekers. There are a lot of them around. They don't know quite what they're after, but they are looking for something. That's the first principle.

This change in priority will affect the whole of our church life. If we say our concern is to reach lost and seeking people, and we don't just want to slot into old traditional ways as we have done before, it may require a long, hard look at everything we do in the church. There may need to be a lot of rearranging done to change the direction of the church's life. We cannot afford to tack evangelism on as an appendage to the church's main activities. It must come back into the centre of things, which may mean other things have to go. We are very good at paying lip service to this and agreeing that it really is important. The test comes when sacrifice has to be made in order to make it possible. It is not good enough for it to remain a good idea. If there is no cost, then probably nothing is actually being done and we have managed to avoid any serious move forward in impacting our world with the gospel.

2. Build relationships of integrity

The second principle is that we have to build relationships of integrity with non-Christian people. Most people who have been Christians for more than two years have very few friends who are not Christians. That's a very sad fact, but it's true. Therefore, it takes an effort and we really have to try hard. We have to stop doing certain things in order to concentrate on building relationships with people who are not yet Christians. But they must be relationships of integrity which are based on the fact that we want them to come to dinner because we care about them. We know that God loves them and we just want to invite them into our lives so that we can allow something of Jesus to touch their lives through us. There's no hidden agenda, because love doesn't have a hidden agenda. The agenda is that you love and care and there may well be some opportunity to talk of Jesus. As I mentioned earlier, some people back off this because they feel they might have the wrong motivation for getting to know non-Christians. There can never be a more loving attitude than a desire to see people saved. If your ulterior motive was to get them to join an organisation or club, it would be very underhand. If you want to see them saved from a lost eternity, how can that possibly be a wrong motivation?

The starting point is making an effort to build relationships with non-Christian people. Some people are put off because they don't know how they would talk to people about their faith. My observation is that if you get the relationship going, God will find ways to open up the subject. If your faith is real, those who get to know you will discover it pretty quickly.

I'm afraid to say that it starts with the leadership of the church. It starts with house-group leaders and everyone else in leadership. You cannot ask people to do what you are not willing to do yourself. It means all of us giving time and energy to it.

3. Know what to say

Thirdly, we need to know how to verbalise our faith in a simple and jargon-free way.

I can remember many years ago, just after I became a Christian, I was a student in London and I lived in a flat in Shepherd's Bush with some friends. It was a typical student type of flat and we used to have regular parties for other medical students and nurses, and they were fairly noisy sorts of affairs. I remember vividly one of these parties; it was quite late at night and we were just standing around and I'd had quite a few glasses of something or other to drink. (Please note that I said I hadn't been a Christian very long!) We'd eaten a lot of food and the party was going well with loud music and everything, and I was enjoying myself. I can remember, almost as if it were yesterday, a girl from our group looking at me and saying, 'Nick, you're a Christian, aren't you?'

I said that I was and she replied, 'Tell me, what does it actually mean to be a Christian?'

'My head was a bit befuddled and my mind was somewhere else and I sort of stuttered something.

Why do I remember that? I remember it because I made a promise to myself that night on two counts. First, I was never going to allow myself, because of alcoholic drink or anything else, to be in a state of mind whereby I was unable to talk coherently and clearly to somebody about my faith. That girl asked a serious question and I was unable to give her a good answer. Secondly, if anybody asked me that question again I would know exactly what to say. It was an important question. It wasn't just a throw-away comment. She wasn't getting at me. She wanted to know. And I don't think she ever heard a coherent answer from me and I owed that to her.

Most opportunities to share like that come when you're not expecting them. Somebody out of the blue says something and you think, 'I should have prepared for this.' Now is the time to prepare for it, because there are people who are dying spiritually, who are going to ask you how they can know God and how they can find life. You need to know what to say. Do you know what you will say at that given moment in time? Will it be just a pat answer full of clichés? Most people can spot that and don't like it. At the very least, we should be confident that when the occasion arises, we will know what to say in a way that is simple and easy to understand, even if it is just a word of personal testimony.

4. A safe place

Fourthly, we need to provide a place so that people can hear a dangerous message in a safe environment. It needs to be stated again and again that the prime place for personal witness is out in the world from Monday to Saturday. The real task of the church begins on Monday at work. Sunday is a place of gathering, but it is out in the ordinariness of life that the church must function as salt and light. Nevertheless, recognising this to be true, having shared with someone in the week, we may feel we want to invite them along to something. Since there may not be a special event coming up, and the Sunday service is the most regular event, why not bring them there? But, as we have seen, that is where the difficulty lies for so many—they cannot bring non-Christian friends to church because either they don't consider it very safe, or it is embarrassingly boring. I don't believe we should ditch everything we do in church, but we can at least try to provide a good and relatively safe environment for people to hear a very dangerous message —the message of the gospel. We do not have to restrict the moving of the Spirit or the sense of life, vitality and joy that many of us have found, but we do need to treat people with respect.

It may well be that many are not yet ready to come to a church service and we should be providing a safe place for them mid-week. When you ask some people to come to church to hear the Christian message, you are actually asking them to cross two barriers at the same time. The first, which may interest them, is to hear about Christ, but emotionally they may well not yet be ready for the presumed commitment to church. Therefore, they may well turn down the offer. We might make a big mistake if we assume they are turning down the opportunity to hear the gospel, when in fact it is the thought of going to church on a Sunday that is the problem. Many people already have a family routine worked out for Sunday and are in no hurry to break it. In Britain, we probably need to open up the possibility of weekday outreach as much as a Sunday. Then, in people's minds, we are not asking for them to take too big a step all at once. The Alpha course, pioneered by Holy Trinity, Brompton, has been very successful, partly because it provides such an event. This is a basic eight to ten week course for those wanting to examine the Christian faith in a relaxed atmosphere. It gives opportunity to listen and to discuss without pressure. Others have discovered different things, including evangelistic Bible studies, discussion groups or evangelistic-style meetings.

C.H. Spurgeon made this observation:

> A curious circumstance came under my notice lately. It seems

> that men may come to hear a preacher on a week evening with less suspicion than on the Sunday. One who had attended a week-night service was asked to come on the Sabbath, but replied, 'Oh, no; I have not gone so far as that yet!' Attendance at a place of worship on the Sunday has in London become to many people a profession of religion. Merely to hear Spurgeon on a Thursday is a different matter.

But there will also be many who will feel they would like to come to church. It is a tremendously good discipline to examine what we do and say there, and find out how much or little of it actually relates. The terrifying truth is that a lot of what we do does not even relate to Christians, let alone non-Christians. Up to now, we may not have dared to challenge it, but if we are not going to become increasingly irrelevant, we had better examine ourselves. We use words and phrases that are just in-jargon. It is an alarming thing to listen to the average church service (and new churches are as bad as everyone else) and notice how much that is said makes no sense whatever to the person who does not normally attend. We must either issue a phrase book to everyone who comes, or do something about changing things. Our behaviour is strange, to say the least. A friend of mine put his hand up in the service and his non-Christian friend didn't know whether he wanted to ask a question or go to the toilet!

Some in the (so-called) charismatic churches have believed that the only way to know the power of God is to sing choruses, endlessly repeated, for hours. I love to sing and worship God in that way, but we are in danger of making terrible presumptions about how God works. To ask seeking people to stand for hours and sing songs they don't know, in the hope that they will sense the presence of God, is incredibly inconsiderate. If we want to have seeking people in our churches, the key to helping them is plenty of explanation. You can get away with a lot if you show you care and understand, and take the time and trouble to say so. It is all a question of priority. If you consider outsiders a secondary issue and to be tolerated, then you will lose them. If you help them to realise that you understand how they are feeling; that you are not wanting to pressurise them and are thrilled they are there, they will keep coming.

Many people have begun to run their services to be visitor friendly. Of course, it means you will probably have to put on other meetings for the body of the committed people to get together. If you come to the conclusion that Sunday morning or evening is the best time for unsaved people to visit, it will challenge your priorities as a church as to whether those folk are to be given first pick and the believers meet at another time instead. My experience is that if you try to make your services free of cringe factors and understandable to most normal people, and if you explain what is going on and teach on issues of life that will help Christians and non-Christians alike, you will find that not only will people want to bring friends, but they are amazed at how much they are benefiting themselves.

To begin to reshape services can easily give the impression that you believe evangelism is getting people into the church building. Of course it isn't that, as the heart of reaching the lost is to go out to where they are. But at the end of the day, you are hoping they will come to something that enables them to meet Jesus in the context of the church body. It is then vital that the cultural gap is not so large that they cannot cross it. The church must never take on the values of the world, but it must speak in the language of its generation. We are in danger of providing such a big cultural gap for non-Christians to cross that they never get to the real issue of facing Jesus, because the church gets in the way. We must do everything we can to speak to our generation in a way that they can understand.

The tension of restraint

Some who want to make their services more available to outsiders may struggle with fitting together what they have learned and experienced about the moving of the Spirit with what they want to do to be more accessible to non-churched people. They may well have been encouraged that to have signs and wonders of one sort or another in the service is the way to demonstrate the presence of God, and that people will be touched by the dramatic things that happen. Others believe the service should be like a performance and presented from the front, with very little participation.

We must realise that all those who have much to teach us have their own history and are the product of their own experience and pilgrimage. We do well to be challenged by different ones, but find our own way forward in the detail. In my own experience, I believe that the church in Willow Creek in Chicago has prophetically challenged us to question whether or not we really do want to prioritise the lost. Having decided that, then we have to ask what we are going to do about it. We must learn everything we can from others, and then see how we can make these things effective in our own culture and environment. If we are going to find the best path, we must be prepared to be very honest with ourselves and ready to change if need be, in order to be more effective. There is no point in telling non-Christians what they ought or ought not to respond to. We had better live in reality. Most of us would do well not to presume but to find out the truth.

For my part, I have become aware that as we have tried to discover new freedoms in our worship, not only are we in danger of becoming more culturally distant, but also of creating a place where the church members, while enjoying the services, find it a difficult environment to invite friends to. They are afraid of the unpredictability, and fear that something will happen that would seriously embarrass them in front of their friends. So, for the sake of the outsiders, we may have to sacrifice something of what we enjoy in order to help others find Jesus. We want to keep the sense of life, but we have to do things in a way that helps non-Christians not only to feel they are welcome but also that they are included.

In our experience, we have concluded that although the average non-Christian does not sing much, some joy-filled and meaningful singing is attractive to them, as it expresses something of the life we have found. If non-Christians were in the majority, it would be foolish to sing too much. The key is they don't feel that they have come to an in-club and are therefore made to feel like outsiders. Explanation, explanation and explanation are the three key things!

It also needs to be said that those with a religious background and those who have some sort of church experience will respond differently to those who have embraced a very secular framework to life. The former may really appreciate the vibrant singing and expressions of joy, whereas the latter may be more at home with a presented format. Nothing will suit everyone and therefore a variety of approaches will help.

I would say that in our experience of 'seeker events', we have at times gone too far in trying to make things 'acceptable', and in so doing have been in danger of not allowing people to be impacted by the presence of the living Jesus. We were denying what we had received through the renewal of the Spirit, rather than finding a framework through which seekers could be most easily opened up to an encounter with him.

The key is in not allowing *a principle* to become *a method*.

We all like method because it makes us feel secure, but it usually kills things off. Other people may appear to be successful in what they do, so we tend to try and copy it, assuming the secret to be a method instead of looking at the principle and applying it within our context. We can also see something that works well and fail to understand that it has as much to do with the anointed gift of a person as with the way they do things.

Here are some things we have begun to find useful:

(a) Visual arts are extremely powerful when done well, and they can be great vehicles for the Spirit. When done badly, they can create the opposite effect! They do not work well as isolated items, but in serving the whole, and primarily serving the preaching of the word, they are very effective. Songs, drama, dance or video can all increase the effectiveness of what is communicated. These art forms have the added benefit of releasing many gifts in the body that may otherwise remain dormant.

(b) If these are to work well, they need to flow together. When presented as items introduced by an MC, they turn the whole thing into a show and it loses its power.

(c) Expect the Holy Spirit to touch people at any point in the service. He can move upon people through anything that is offered to him.

(d) Aim for excellence in everything you do.

(e) Watch out for in-speak (referring to people and situations that only a certain number of people know about). This isolates new people.

(f) Continually check language and phrases. Avoid jargon which is understood only by Christians who have got into that way of speaking.

(g) Keep reviewing to discover if what you are doing is driving people away or attracting them to stay. Note that we can never water down the gospel, but we can present it in ways that most people understand.

5. Prayer

Fifthly, we're to be disciplined in the area of prayer. That's at the heart of everything we do. I will say more about this later on.

6. Meeting together

Sixthly, we must not neglect to meet together for worship, prayer, praise and teaching. If we are to have meetings that are welcoming to those not yet converted, we will need to provide other times for the Christians to be together for their own up-building. This may be in small groups in homes, in celebration meetings or in both.

In the book of Hebrews, the writer wrote to the early church because something was happening in the church which was most disturbing. The writer said this: 'Let us not neglect to meet together as is the habit of some, but rather let us encourage one another.' At each opportunity we need to make every effort to be there when the church gathers together. This is because we need to be a source of encouragement to one another. We must not neglect this.

The difficulty is that many people are so incredibly busy. Also, family life is of supreme importance and in the past families have been badly damaged by one or other of the parents being out at too many meetings. I know that Jesus did not come that we might have meetings and have them more abundantly. But having said that, we must recognise we are part of a 'take it or leave it' generation. It is a responsibility of the leadership to make sure there are not endless meetings; that no individual is doing too many jobs; that there is plenty of time for family life; that the church does not become yet another major stress factor in people's lives.

However, the writer to the Hebrews had a very good

reason for saying what he did. If you neglect to meet together, not only will you suffer, but you will be a source of discouragement to others. When we meet together, both in celebration as well as in small groups, we come to encourage one another, to strengthen each other and to support one another as we live in an alien world.

There are home-group leaders who will identify with the fact that it is incredibly discouraging when people are casual about house groups and don't bother to come, or don't even bother to ring to say they are not coming. Every time you turn up to house group, you encourage somebody. Just by your presence you are likely to encourage them, regardless of what you do. Do not neglect meeting together. There are people who are tempted to opt out of mainstream church life and to stay on the fringe. If you know anything about warfare, you'll know where the enemy hits first. He will always hit the fringe; the person who's at the back of the line.

There are many people who are casual about meeting on a Sunday, and they opt out of house group, or they come when they feel like it. What happens? The enemy finds them. If you stay on the fringe you become most vulnerable. We must encourage one another not to neglect meeting together with the church, because this is the place of encouragement and strength. It's out of this that we go into the world.

To belong to a body is vital. We were made for body life. You hear some people say that they belong to the universal body and that they do not need to be part of a particular church. I would be wary of such an attitude. It may well mean that they are unwilling to be accountable to anyone and are a law unto themselves.

7. Use your gifts

Seventhly, we are to use our giftedness for the sake of the body of Christ. Every one of us is gifted. Every one of us should be using our gifts in the body of Christ. There's no place for passengers. In a human body there are no parts without a function—every part does something. Find something to do. In any church there are always so many things to be done, and usually such a lot is done by the few.

The trouble is that some jobs seem more spiritual than others. Every job is important if it enables the local church to function better. It might be putting out the chairs, helping with the children or getting the PA set up. I don't know what it might happen to be, but everyone should find an area of church life to be committed to.

Imagine someone asking you, 'What are you doing in the church? What is your function in the body and how are you helping?' None of us should be able to turn round and say, 'I'm not doing anything.' When everybody is doing something the whole body moves together. Use your giftedness.

It is important to note the difference between natural gifts and spiritual gifts. The first can be a great service to the church, as well as a major problem. A person who has a natural gift which they are using in their job, may not be so effective if they try and put the same principles to work in the church. An accountant who spends his whole week helping people to save and not spend money, may find it very difficult to be generous with the church's money! In the area of spiritual gifts, we often need other people to help us recognise them. When we are aware of the gifts God has given us, we must not neglect to use them, but have them continually stirred up and used for the benefit of the body.

The main reason why so many are frustrated in the

church is that they don't know how God has made them and have not discovered their area of gifting. Many are working hard, but in an area where they are not gifted and so become tired and lose their drive to carry on. In the past, we have tended to start with a list of jobs that need doing and then tried to fill them with willing people. We have got to begin with the people and help them discover what they do well and what they enjoy doing and therefore will continue to do, even when times get hard. Then we should match them up with the specific areas of responsibility within the church. If we believe that the Holy Spirit gives the gifts in the church, then if we take this approach, not only will we end up with satisfied people and a church that functions well, but we will be amazed that there is a wonderful variety in every body of people.

It is well worth noting the example of two young men, Stephen and Philip, who made a tremendous impact in the early church. They started out serving at tables. It is often the case that when someone has a desire to serve, finds what needs doing and gets on with it, they grow into the main areas of work that God has for them.

We are so quick to find one another's weaknesses, as if there was something wrong with having weaknesses. Of course there isn't. They are a gift of God! We need other people to fill the gaps created by our weaknesses. We must not train people in the area of their weakness, but in the area of their strength. Most of us were not made to be all-rounders. Body life means we all have strengths to contribute. The exciting thing is to help one another find them and then rejoice in one another.

In summary:

1. Make a decision that non-Christian people not only matter to God, but they matter to us.
2. Build relationships of integrity with them.

3. Know how to share your faith with others in a way that isn't pat and trite, but is real and sincere.

4. Provide safe places for non-Christians to hear the good news in a way they can understand and that gives them time.

5. Pray at every opportunity as a sign of your utter dependence on the Lord.

6. Give time to meet together to encourage and build one another up. Be a courage giver and not a courage taker.

7. Find your giftedness and look for a place for it to be used in the body as a service to others.

If we take these steps, we may well find that as a church we are more effective in reaching our friends and neighbours and in seeing them become integrated members of the body as well.

Another approach

There also has to be some less familiar and less natural forms of evangelism if we are going to make a full impact on our communities. There are many groups of people, particularly in city life, that will require different means of evangelism from those already discussed, in order for us to reach them.

For example, in some of the housing estates or tower blocks where people may have little contact with Christians on a day-to-day basis, we need to find more direct means in order to penetrate these unreached areas. In some of these areas, we have to use more unfamiliar forms of evangelism in order to break the ground. It would be good to see more people involved in street work and visiting homes. This does not have to be done in an aggressive way. Nor do we need to be put off because of other religious groups who do the same thing. The difference with us should be that we have come to give something, and not to receive. How wonderful if we can leave something of the gospel in each home, whether in the form of literature, a video or through offering to pray for a need in the home and releasing a miracle. Not many of the other groups will be doing that. In a world where everyone expects you to be on the make, it is quite revolutionary to find a group of people who want nothing except to bring help and hope.

We may well need to find more unusual methods, without missing out on the normal and more familiar.

The people who need to hear about Jesus are almost certainly near to you. You've been with some of them this week. You already know them. You've seen them. They are not far away. For many of them the time is now and the means to tell them is a natural means, but you've still got to take another step in order to bring them into that sphere where they can open up to you and you can open up to them.

Jesus cares about lost people. He loves the church and he is with us. We're going to spend eternity with him and with one another. That is a fact. The priority at this time between now and when we go to be with the Lord is that we must give our energies to reaching unchurched non-Christian people and sharing our faith with them. We must not neglect to be together. We must be together for worship and teaching, but there's a world outside that needs to meet Jesus. These people must become a priority in our lives. It was the last thing he told us to do, and when he comes back we want to be found doing that very same thing.

I do not believe there is any place at all for debate on this issue. There's plenty of room for debate on how we should run our services and on what we should and shouldn't do in order to find the best means to reach people. The issue of whether or not we should prioritise the lost is not up for debate. It's not an issue to be discussed, because Jesus told us to do it. The real issue is not that. The real issue is the attitude of our hearts.

I know that what I struggle with deep inside is the disease which I think can only be described as a hardness of heart. I can think of a reason why I'm afraid to talk to this person, afraid to talk to that one. I can think of many, many excuses. But I have to say that the greatest problem I have is a hardness of heart—a hardness of heart towards lost people. I'm not sure how much I really care. I'll be honest with you. My prayer at the moment is the prayer of the song, 'Soften my heart, Lord.' I may not know what to do, I may not know what to say, I may not have any idea how to go about sharing my faith, but I want to have a heart that is soft enough to care.

I want to have the attitude of heart that when I see and meet people who aren't Christians—when I'm talking to them, whether it's at work on Monday morning, on the bus, or in a shop—something inside me cares about them and their relationship with God. I hope you can appreciate what I'm trying to say. My prayer is, 'Lord, will you soften my heart?'

Soften my heart, Lord, soften my heart.
From all indifference set me apart.
To feel your compassion, to weep with your tears.
Come soften my heart, O Lord, soften my heart.

I don't want to be like the disciples who had gone off for lunch. I want to be like Jesus who saw a woman at a well and realised that here was a woman in need. This very week, I don't want to miss the people Jesus brings into my life. It's easy to talk about it and have read nice books about it all and say, 'That was another challenging book or talk. Now what is next?' I do not want to fall into that trap. I want to be part of a body of people who are saying to God, 'We're not quite sure what to do, Lord, but we want to care. We want to go down trying. Even if we make a terrible mess of the whole thing, Lord, at the end of the day we want to be a church who at least had a go, and who at least said that we want to care about your world. If, Lord, your heart is broken for the people of this world, then we want to say, "We're on your side. We're with you whatever the cost. We want to help you touch lost people with the good news."'

8

The Source of Power

Whatever changes we make in the church—however we alter things, however we improve the standard of our music and drama and try to make our meetings visitor friendly—nothing of effect will happen unless we understand the source of power. The world is not changed by good techniques, although the church would do well not to label everything that smacks of good methodology as worldly. It certainly does not work merely to look and see how God is blessing a church elsewhere and assume that if we apply the same things in our own situation we will receive the same blessing. Having said that, we need to learn as much as we possibly can from each other, understanding principles rather than mere method.

Watchman Nee once illustrated the point by saying that if you go into a room and find there is a table lamp and it isn't working properly, then, in order to rectify the situation, you could change the bulb, but it still might not work. You could clean the lampshade and it still would not work. You could check the fuse and it still might not work. 'What I would suggest you do,' he said, 'is look for the source of power in the room and plug it in.'

If we're really going to see God touch and change people's lives as we want to, then we must concentrate on the source of power and make sure we are plugged in to that source. It would be totally wrong for us to be looking at the whole issue of reaching the lost without coming to the heart of the matter, and that is the need to pray. I do believe that the great need today is for revival. Revival is closely linked to prayer. But if we pray for revival and do nothing, we are not only being disobedient, but we are also misunderstanding how spiritual awakening comes. If John Wesley had sat at home waiting for revival, he might still be waiting today! But in all of our activity, if we are not looking to God for something far greater than we are at present experiencing, then we will be content with the little we have and not see the far greater purposes God has for us.

It also needs to be said, as I mentioned earlier, that the release of power is so much greater when there is unity in the body. We are going to see large urban areas impacted with the gospel in a far greater way when the church moves in unity. This is not the same thing at all as a group of ministers meeting together to plan a united event. That may be good, but it isn't the unity God desires or requires. It has to get to the point where leaders actually see themselves as part of one church, deal ruthlessly with envy, competition and suspicion and share their gifts and resources. There may be many congregations, but as far as God is concerned, there is only one church in the city or town. If we only pay lip service to that truth, we will be weak. When we move together, maintaining our distinctives but rejoicing in our oneness, we will pray with great power and authority.

Prayer, like evangelism, may be one of those words we wish we could change. It would be good to change the word 'evangelism' because it speaks to most of us of a rather aggressive 'go and get them' type of activity. The problem with the word 'prayer' is that as soon as you mention it, then psychologically it has a sort of sleepifying effect on you. You begin to think, 'This is rather boring and irrelevant', and you feel dozy. For example, if this chapter was called 'Prayer and the Local Church', many would just skip it thinking they'd heard it all before, even if they were not doing it. Unfortunately, that's the connotation prayer has. So many prayer meetings we've known in the past have been boring and dull. We've heard the same people pray rather long prayers and it's all become a rather negative thing.

Let me share a few observations that have encouraged me in this area.

1. What is it that stands out about men and women in the Old Testament who achieved great things? If you bring to mind some of the people God has used, such as Abraham, Moses, Daniel, David, Nehemiah and the prophets, and you recall many of the amazing things these very ordinary people achieved, I wonder what stands out in your mind about them?

When I think of them I think of two things: one is that these were very ordinary people with very real weaknesses. They are very transparent characters. They are like you and me. There's a lovely passage in James 5 where it says: 'The prayer of a righteous man is powerful and effective. Elijah was a man just like us.' Isn't that encouraging? Of course, most of us do not think for a minute that it could be true.

We think, 'Oh no, he was Elijah, the great prophet.' But it is as if God is saying to us, 'I know him. I watched him every day. I saw how difficult it was for him to get out of bed in the morning. I saw the conflicts in his mind. I smelt his socks. I know what he's like. He's just like the rest of you, and look what he did.'

On the one hand, we are aware of the weakness of these ordinary human beings, and on the other hand, we cannot escape the fact that these were all individuals who spent time talking to God. When Abraham was concerned about Sodom, he went to God and discussed the people of the city with him. Moses talked to God about the children of Israel. Daniel was a man who prayed three times a day and eventually he was put in the lions' den because of it. He was a man who was consistent in spending time talking to God. Nehemiah, who rebuilt the walls of Jerusalem, was a man who prayed. David was a man continually praying. The prophets were men who knew God. Time and time again you see these two things together: human weakness but a sense of the need of God to work in their lives. And when those two things were combined, these ordinary human beings did extraordinary things.

When you look through the Old Testament, in particular the book of Judges, you find the children of Israel continually sinning against God and disobeying him. Then you find a consistent theme that runs something like this: 'The people of God cried unto the Lord and the Lord sent them a deliverer.' God answered their prayers. What stands out about these people is that they were people who were rewarded with acts of God's power when they had a heart to look to God for help.

2. This is even more obvious in the New Testament. It is most noticeably seen in the life and ministry of Jesus. For example, as you read through the book of Luke, you find that time after time, even in the middle of his busy life, Jesus withdrew to pray. We read in Luke 3 how, on the occasion when the Holy Spirit came down on him, Jesus was praying. Another time, when the crowds were gathered all around him and he was at the height of his popularity, he stopped preaching and went off alone to pray. Another time he was out all night praying and then he came back and chose his disciples. It was as he was praying that he was transfigured before them. On yet another occasion, he was praying and miracles started to happen. It's an interesting exercise to study the prayer life of Jesus, but what is so striking is this: here is Jesus, the one

man you would think doesn't need to pray because he's God, and yet his life is a life of continuous prayer.

It happened in different ways and different times. We can easily take one verse and say, 'Jesus prayed all night, therefore we should,' or, 'Jesus got up early to pray, therefore we should all get up early to pray.' I think we can make a law out of something that isn't really there. But Jesus was a man who continually saw that the source of his authority and power was not in himself, but in his relationship with the Father. Yes, he was God, but he needed the Father and the Holy Spirit, and that divine combination of dependence enabled him to do what he did.

It is striking to consider the parables of Jesus. On a number of occasions he taught about prayer. We have the Lord's Prayer because the disciples were so taken with the impact of prayer in his life that they asked him to teach them to pray.

He talked about a widow nagging a judge. He used the story to teach them to be persistent in prayer. He must have known how quickly we would grow weary and give up. Another time he said, 'Ask, and it will be given to you...' and, 'If two of you on earth agree about anything you ask for, it will be done for you by my Father in heaven.'

Time and time again, Jesus taught about prayer because he wanted his disciples to grasp that the heart of getting to know God and discovering his power in their lives, both personally and corporately, is that they learned to pray. No wonder the disciples came to him and said, 'Jesus, teach us to pray.' We really need to be people who know how to pray.

3. Then there is the Acts of the Apostles. What do you find there?

In Acts 1, the great Day of Pentecost when the Holy

Spirit fell, 3,000 people were converted. Where were the disciples? They were gathering together and almost certainly, praying.

In Acts 2 the new Christians gathered together. What were they doing? They were praying. The Lord was adding daily to their number.

In Acts 4 they were in a bit of trouble, and were thrown into jail. There was a bit of hassle going on, so what did they do? They started to pray, and God intervened.

In Acts 9 Ananias was sent to lay hands on Saul of Tarsus who had just been converted. He went to see him and what did he do? He found a man who was praying and as he prayed the Holy Spirit came down upon him.

In Acts 10 Cornelius was praying and God sent an angel.

In Acts 12 Peter was in prison and people were praying. Peter was released.

In Acts 16 Paul went to Philippi. The first place he went to is where people were praying because he wanted to pray for the city to meet other people who prayed.

What do you notice about the life of Jesus? What do you notice about the early church? What do you notice about the teaching of Paul? There is such a clear pattern here. Paul teaches us not to be anxious about anything but in everything, with thanksgiving by prayer and supplication, to make our requests known to God.

4. What can we learn from a study of past revivals? Edwin Orr has researched as thoroughly as anyone into the revival experience, and has followed the patterns throughout church history. His conclusion has been that every revival is different. Every great move of the Holy Spirit is different, but there is one consistent factor, and that is that in every expression of what could be called 'revival' he found what he termed 'unusual prayer'. In other words, in places where the Holy Spirit has moved in powerful ways, it had been preceded and accompanied by

unusual prayer. In the Hebridian revival in the 1950s, hundreds of people were converted in a matter of days across the island. Extraordinary stories are told about men out in the fields working, suddenly falling on their faces before God and being converted. One of the things that was later discovered was that there were two elderly ladies, one aged eighty-six and the other aged eighty-four, one of whom was blind, who had met together day after day to pray for revival in the Hebrides. Then suddenly God began to work. The Welsh revivals followed the same pattern, although in each situation the outworking was different.

5. The same is true if you look at present-day revivals. In many parts of the world, the church is growing at a remarkable rate. In each situation there are a number of factors that have made certain nations so remarkably open to the gospel. Even if there are sociological phenomena as well, the most common factors are the boldness of believers to share their faith and the centrality of prayer. These situations are characterised by the presence of people who believe that only God can open people up to respond to the gospel.

Most of us know about the church in Korea. We have heard something about Yongi Cho's church of 700,000 people. The largest Methodist church and the largest Presbyterian church are found in the city of Seoul. There are many massive churches in Korea. But if you look at each of those churches you'll find the same thing: these people have an extraordinary awareness of the need of prayer. They take it very seriously. Why? Because they want to see their nation impacted and believe the source of power is God himself.

Look at South America. What is the common factor in the revivals that have broken out in Argentina, Brazil, Chile, Guatemala and other countries? When we see these extraordinary moves of the Spirit of God and we take a closer look, we find that at the back of it all people have learned to pray. They've discovered the source of power.

If we look at the lives of men and women in the Old Testament, what do we notice about them? What is central to the ministry of Jesus? What do we find when we look at the teaching of Jesus? What strikes us about the Acts of the Apostles or the teaching of Paul? What do we observe about past revivals? What happens when we look at revivals of the present? If we look at all these things together, there is a consistent factor which cannot be denied. It is that all these people have learned that there is a key. The key is God. They have actually learned that the source of power, the only way people's lives can be changed, is by the intervention of God himself and not by the cleverness of human beings. And the way to bring that about is through prayer.

It's easy to think that all these people prayed, so prayer is the answer. Prayer isn't the answer. Prayer has never been the answer. God is the answer, but the means by which God responds and works on earth is through prayer. It is as human beings pray that God begins to move.

6. Why is it that in the main there is such a lack of real spiritual vitality in the Western church? Would it be right to suggest that it is because as Westerners we are locked into a materialistic viewpoint which pushes us to prioritise the physical and the seen as opposed to the spiritual and unseen? We actually believe that activity will win the day and because this is a dominant fact of Western life, it is expressed in our church life. Do we fundamentally believe that by much activity, doing things and having things we shall get the job done? At the heart of it all we are materialistically minded. In the East, it is understood much more that in reality it is the spiritual world, that affects the

natural world, and not the other way round. We have to change our thinking radically if we're really going to see something happen here in the West.

As we look around us at the evidence in other parts of the world, we would have to admit that if we really want to see cities changed and people coming to Christ in large numbers, then the secret must be a release of the power of God in response to heartfelt prayer.

9
Why on Earth Pray?

Why should we pray? I would like to suggest seven reasons.

1. We pray because we want to get to know him

The heart of the Christian experience is having God as a friend. How can you have a friend you never spend time with? The mark of a real friend is that you spend time with him or her. The most profound challenge to most of us as Christians is to realise how little time we actually, consciously spend talking with Jesus. I know that in one sense we spend every day with Jesus. But I wonder how often in our spare moments—lunch time, on the way to work or early in the morning or evening—we consciously spend time just talking with Jesus. How do you get to know a person if you don't spend time with him?

I've been a Christian for more than twenty years. The hardest thing in my Christian life is actually to spend time praying. You'll hear people give glib talks about how great their prayer life is, but so much is unreal because most of us know that it is a struggle. We find it very difficult because we're activity orientated. We want to get on and do something. Yet it is our relationship with Jesus which makes the whole of life worthwhile.

There is the most amazing statement made about a

man's life in Genesis 5. We are told: 'Altogether, Enoch lived 365 years. Enoch walked with God; then he was no more, because God took him away.' I can think of no greater thing to be said about a person than, 'He walked with God.' The Bible does not tell us what he actually did for all that time, but we can be sure he did what he was meant to do. When you walk with God, you do what you should and no more. What an experience for your whole life to be one long walk in the company of God. Surely prayer starts here. We can get things from a machine, but God is to be known. When prayer primarily has an agenda it misses the point. It may develop into asking, but it begins with being.

2. We pray to humble ourselves and express our utter dependence on God

When you start to pray, you are admitting, 'I can't do it.' Most of us are rather proud. You remember as a child, time and time again your parents asked if they could help you and you said, 'No, I can do it.' They knew perfectly well you couldn't and you knew you couldn't, but you were blowed if you were going to say so. When we start to pray we are actually saying, 'I cannot do it. I can't face today. I can't do what I'm called to do and I need supernatural help.' We humble ourselves and admit that we have a need. A man who prays is a man who admits he has a need. If we don't pray, the truth is that we actually believe we can do it; with enough effort we can make it work.

3. When we pray, we align ourselves with God's will

Things happen on earth when God's will and our will actually lock into one another. That is the secret of the power of God. When your will and God's will lock into one another, in some remarkable way God is able to work. We so often assume that prayer is this: we know what we want and what is best, and prayer is the means by which we pursuade God to fit into our will. So, in other words, prayer is getting God to change his mind. That is a misunderstanding of biblical prayer.

Prayer, in fact, enables us to have our mind changed to fit into God's will. It's when we pray that we understand God's mind and God's heart and will. We start to lock into that and God says, 'At last! Now we're working together, we can get something done.' It isn't changing God's mind. It is changing our mind and changing our will. It's bringing us in line with God. It is a mystery as to why, but it does seem that God is free to work on earth as we open the door for him to work in the lives of other human beings. His desire to save people is far greater than ours will ever be.

When you pray you begin to say, 'God, what do you want to do and how do you want to do it? I want to go your way.' Yet so often we go to God and say, 'Now, God, I've got an agenda and you need to change this and that in order for it to happen.' It is as if God says to us, 'Excuse me, you've come to the wrong place. This is not a slot machine. This is a relationship where I am the Master and you are the servant. Come to me and listen to me. Listen to what I want to do.'

4. We pray to open a window for the Holy Spirit

This is a very strange thing. Isn't it an amazing thing that the all-powerful God who comes to us by his Holy Spirit has in some way limited himself here on earth and requires us to open a window or a door for him? It is humbling to think that God initiates the prayer as well as everything else. Of course, that still leaves human responsibility to respond to his leading, but this seems to be the way in which the New Testament indicates God operates. That's why he has called us to pray. In the simple act of human prayer there is a sense in which we open the way for the Holy Spirit to act. But if our free will is submitted to God, then his Spirit can begin to move as we pray in accordance with his will. In Acts 4, we read that they prayed God would fill them with boldness. At the end of the prayer, the place in which they met was shaken by the Holy Spirit. It's one of those prayers that you get the impression God heard!

They prayed and the Holy Spirit began to move. The two things were dovetailed together. They began to pray and as they prayed, asking the Holy Spirit to come, the building started to shake. The Holy Spirit is longing to come, waiting to come, but he's waiting for human openness; an invitation to come and move among us.

5. Prayer enables angelic activity to be released

An understanding of angelic activity is such a fantastic thing. We need more teaching on the reality of angels. If you're a New Testament believer you must believe in angels. Right the way through the New Testament, as in the Old, angels keep appearing. We can assume that because angels are sent to minister to the saints, and we're the saints, then there must have already been a lot of angelic activity in our lives. We are told to be hospitable because we might entertain an angel unawares. The Bible would not say that if it was not possible. It's very likely that many people, even this week, have had a direct confrontation or meeting with an angel in some way or other.

We read it in the Bible as if it were commonplace. It's amazing how casually we read that an angel came and spoke to someone and then we just move on to the next verse. Really it should excite us, because it is so incredible. If angels were active in the New Testament, surely they are active today.

The Bible gives us some clues as to what angels do. First, they come to minister on our behalf; to serve us in a whole variety of ways. Secondly, they come to fight, as they are warring beings. They fight on our behalf in the heavenly realms. In the book of Daniel, we read that Daniel prayed and then eventually, after a period of time, an angel came to him. The angel explained that the delay in his coming was not that he hadn't left immediately, but that he had been tied up in a conflict, and that Michael had come and sorted his opponent out and then he was free to come to help Daniel. It is quite clear that the moment he prayed, God sent an angel.

In Acts 10, we are told that Cornelius was praying and God sent an angel to him. And again in Acts 12, we read that Peter was put in prison, and the disciples gathered together for prayer. In response to their prayers, an angel came and unlocked Peter from prison. Then Peter came out, knocked on the door where they were praying, but they could hardly believe it was true.

They prayed and what happened? An angel was sent. There are many other New Testament examples of this. But isn't it fantastic to know that when we pray something like this happens—there is a release of angels to act on our behalf? They may be sent to do any number of things. It might be in the area of battle, warfare against demons, or it might be to serve us in other ways. Prayer releases angels. It should give us great enthusiasm to pray because every time we pray we can wonder what's going on behind the scenes in response to our prayers. Whenever we pray, there is some unseen activity. Don't you often wish you could see what is going on?

One man was given some real insight. You remember

how Elisha, when the city was surrounded by attacking forces, told his servant who was with him not to worry, as there were more with them than with the enemy. Now, at the time there were only two of them! The lad obviously gave Elisha a strange look. Elisha asked for the servant to have his eyes opened and have a glimpse of the real situation. When the heavens parted, he could see legion upon legion of angels. Elisha knew they were there all along, so he had not been concerned.

Sometimes, I think it would be nice to see them, but I don't know whether we could cope, but we do so need to know that God is active in this way.

6. There is victory in warfare when we pray

Paul says in Ephesians 6 that we need to 'pray at all times', as part of our effective armour in the warfare. In this passage, Paul underlines the necessity to pray for the church as a protection against the enemy. Because there is a battle on for the church, praying for the church is absolutely crucial.

7. We pray because we care

We care for people. Jesus told a parable in which a man came to a house in need of some food. The owner didn't have any, but a friend down the road had plenty. The trouble was that it was midnight. What did he do? He went down the road and he knocked on the door until his friend got up.

Jesus reminds us that people are coming into our lives all the time who are in need. What are they in need of? They are in need of salvation, they need forgiveness, they need the Holy Spirit. We haven't got what they need, but we know who has. What does prayer do? When we pray, we are going to the resources of heaven on behalf of the person who hasn't got them. We become a go-between, because we care. Jesus encourages us to come to him on behalf of others who do not yet know him. Isn't that what prayer is all about? We come on behalf of the lost and we say, 'Jesus, here's a lost person who needs salvation. Will you please give it to him. Here's a needy person; he needs help, so will you please give it to him?'

I was talking to a guy from Ghana who now lives in England. He was saying that when he was in Ghana the entire church of several thousand people was up at 5 am every morning to pray for lost people. He had a valid point to make. He said, 'It's interesting. We saw people converted every day in our church. Now I'm here, people can't even come to one prayer meeting a week, and we practically never see people converted.' He wasn't getting at people, but there was a wistfulness in his voice. He wondered what would happen if the people in his city began to pray like those in Ghana. Maybe he would see exactly the same fruit.

I think that is the challenge to you and me in the church. There are still thousands and thousands of people whom Jesus wants in his kingdom.

As the church meets together, whether it's in the early morning or whether it's in a monthly prayer meeting, whenever it is that we meet, we must give more time to pray.

You do not have to be an Anglican to have a prayer book. Why not have everyone in the church own a small booklet in which they can write down the names of the unsaved people they are praying for? Then encourage them to bring their books to house groups and other gatherings, where they can be regularly sharing the people they are praying for. They could also include some church people to pray for to make sure everyone, especially the leaders, are being prayed for regularly.

Tell Joshua

I am impressed by the fact that after the famous victory of Joshua over the Amalekites, when Moses had been lifting up his hands on the mountain and by so doing had swayed the course of events, God said that they were to write it down to remind them of what happened. Then he said in Exodus 17:14, 'And make sure that Joshua hears it.' As the church today engages in evangelism, it does well to 'hear it' and remember that it is in the place of prayer that the battles are won.

Wilderness or Promised land?

The children of Israel were given a fantastic promise: wherever the soles of their feet would tread, God would give that land to them. Here is partnership. There was no way by they could overcome the inhabitants of the land by their natural ability. It had to be in God's power. But, on the other hand, just to rely on God and stand still would achieve nothing. They had to co-operate and actually go and step onto the land.

In exactly the same way today, there is no way we can win large numbers of men and women to Christ and see communities and cities changed. It must be a work of God. But it will not happen unless we move forward to possess all that God has for us. We cannot sit and wait for revival, any more than we should believe that revival is another name for a great deal of man-centred evangelism. It is a partnership of our obedience and God's power. We can be in no doubt about God's power, but we may have some problems with the obedience side of things.

This could be a very exciting and rewarding time if we will go forward with courage.

But there is also a strong warning here. As they stood on

the banks of the Jordan, on the threshold of receiving what God had prepared for them, the children of Israel had their all-too-painful history to remind them that they had been there before. They had been at the edge before. They had seen into the Promised Land before, but most of their predecessors had failed to go in.

We may have every intention of going forward to enjoy all that God has for us, but if we do not heed the warnings, we will find ourselves in the same predicament—disillusioned and wandering yet again around the wilderness. Almost certainly, nearly every person reading this will have either known of or heard of a church that set out well, but today is a poor shadow of what it once was. The Christian landscape is littered with people and churches that had such promise—a real heart to reach their community with the gospel and express the kingdom of God in the place where they are—but are now struggling to survive. The call came to enter into the land God had given them to possess, and as soon as they decided to go forward, the enemy found the areas of weakness and exploited them. They failed to heed the warnings and learn the lessons of history. We are all capable of being in the same place, and therefore need to be sure of building in the safeguards. Without them we will go forward with great enthusiasm and find ourselves torn apart, both by the enemy without and the enemy within.

What follows in the next few chapters is very different from what has gone before in this book, but it is all part of the same message. If we take one without the other we may end up in trouble, and we may never achieve what God has for us. If we are prepared to heed the warnings and set a guard on the church, we can go forward with confidence that we have done everything we can to make sure we do not find ourselves having begun well and ended in disappointment.

A WARNING

These things happened to them as examples and were written down as warnings for us, on whom the fulfilment of the ages has come (1 Cor 10:11).

Finally, be strong in the Lord and in his mighty power. Put on the full armour of God so that you can take your stand against the devil's schemes (Eph 6:10-11).

Be self-controlled and alert. Your enemy the devil prowls around like a roaring lion looking for someone to devour (1 Pet 5:8).

10

A Warning Has Been Given

I remember meeting someone once who told me that while he had been digging up his garden he had come across an unexploded bomb. In fact he didn't know what it was at first, so he just put it on one side out of harm's way. While his back was turned, the children saw it, picked it up and started to play with it. He was concerned that it might be something dangerous, so he rescued it from the children and rang the police, who came round remarkably quickly! After some investigation, they discovered that the previous owner of the house had come home from the First World War with a mustard gas bomb as a souvenir and he had buried it in the garden. He had forgotten to tell the people to whom he sold the house that it was there. At first, the bomb disposal people were going to blow it up and then they realised it was a gas bomb, so they took it away. In this case a tragedy was avoided. But the story could have been quite different. The amazing thing is that the previous owner forgot to warn them of the danger when so much harm could have been done.

Paul, when writing to the Corinthians, gave the church a clear warning. In 1 Corinthians 10, he explains that what had happened to the children of Israel back in the time of the Exodus had been recorded and written down, not just as a piece of history, but to warn us of the dangers of what could happen if we behaved like they did. It's quite clear that the principles which caused their undoing are potentially here in the church today. In fact, he warns us that if we believe it will not happen to us, we are very likely to be in for trouble.

He was not saying anything in anger; he was just giving his readers a warning. The children of Israel had a destiny, and their destiny was the Promised Land. It is a tragic story that of the million or so people who left Egypt, only a small number ever entered the Promised Land.

The Corinthian Church also had a destiny and Paul was concerned that both individually and corporately they could fail to fulfil their calling. And God has a destiny for his church today.

This passage reminds us that every individual has a God-given destiny and purpose for their lives. God loves us so much that he warns us of the possibility that we may never fulfil the ultimate purpose for which we were made. It would be tragic if we fell short of it or failed to enter into everything that God had prepared for us. So it is with the church as a whole. God has a destiny—not only for the worldwide church, but for each and every individual expression of it. Many churches never fulfil the purpose God has for them because they fail to heed the warnings. These warnings are not negative instructions—they are positive, creative gifts from God. They are meant to steer us on the right course, because God intends us to reach our destination.

I don't know about you, but I want to fulfil everything God has for my life, and I want to be sure of attaining my final destiny in heaven with him. The children of Israel in large measure never reached the destination they were intended for.

In 1 Corinthians 10:1-13 we read:

> For I do not want you to be ignorant of the fact, brothers, that

> our forefathers were all under the cloud and that they all passed through the sea. They were all baptised into Moses in the cloud and in the sea. They all ate the same spiritual food and drank the same spiritual drink; for they drank from the spiritual rock that accompanied them, and that rock was Christ. Nevertheless, God was not pleased with most of them; their bodies were scattered over the desert. Now these things occurred as examples to keep us from setting our hearts on evil things as they did. Do not be idolaters, as some of them were; as it is written: 'The people sat down to eat and drink and got up to indulge in pagan revelry.' We should not commit sexual immorality, as some of them did—and in one day twenty-three thousand of them died. We should not test the Lord, as some of them did—and were killed by snakes. And do not grumble, as some of them did—and were killed by the destroying angel. These things happened to them as examples and were written down as warnings for us, on whom the fulfilment of the ages has come. So, if you think you are standing firm, be careful that you don't fall! No temptation has seized you except what is common to man. And God is faithful; he will not let you be tempted beyond what you can bear. But when you are tempted, he will also provide a way out so that you can stand up under it.

Paul is quite clear that the Old Testament account has been written down for our benefit as we are the people 'on whom the fulfilment of the ages has come'. This is the era of the church. These are the last days, and have been ever since Pentecost. This is the final phase of God's history on earth.

We live in a privileged time and something of great significance is happening in our generation. These passages are written down because time and time again people and churches have started well with great intentions, with clear purposes and plans, with a heart after God, but then failed because warnings were not heeded.

At the end of the above passage Paul makes it clear that the temptations which come upon us are not new. These are not things that have been designed specially for the church today. They've been functioning right from the beginning. They have worked so well that the enemy has been able to trap the people of God, the church, for generation after generation, and he will try the same today. It is important that we understand the context of this well-known quotation: 'No such temptation has taken you but such is common to man, but God will provide....'

The temptations talked about here are those very specific ones that are intended to destroy the church of Jesus Christ. These are the temptations that will prevent us reaching our destiny and our full effectiveness for him. The glorious promise here is that there is always a way out (which we have to look for), so that none of us has to fall. God has made it possible for us to push through and discover victory. There is always a way out, but we have to look for it. If we want to avoid the pitfalls, God has promised us that we will find ways to do so. Paul goes on to say that if we do not believe this refers to us, then we had better be careful because it almost certainly does.

Indeed, the more you think it doesn't, the more it is likely to! If you don't think that these things are affecting you now, look out, because they pretty soon will do. We must open our eyes and see what is going on and be sure to avoid the pitfalls the enemy will put in our path.

Of course, the main reason the children of Israel didn't enter the land was an apparent crisis of faith at the moment they were meant to go in. They chickened out and did not have enough confidence once they saw the giants and the walled cities. But it's too easy to say that it was just a crisis of faith at that particular moment in time. Moments of crisis like these are never what they appear. There is nearly always an accumulation of things, and the crisis situation only serves to demonstrate the weakness that is already there. We fail in the crisis, not because of the event itself, but because in all the intermediary stages along the way we have failed to respond in the way we should. If we respond to God properly in the intermediary stages, then when the major crises come we stand a better chance of responding rightly.

They had opted out of every other miracle up to that point. Whenever there had been a difficulty they had complained and moaned and turned to Moses. And Moses had cried out to God who had done the most remarkable miracles for them. But they never entered into the fullness of those miracles themselves. They were observers and not participants. It was not their faith. It was not their prayer. It was not their expectation that God would provide for them. They had complained, but they had expected Moses to believe for the miracle. Because, up to that point, they had only been observers. When it came to crossing the Jordan and going into the Promised Land, they had no personal experience of God's provision in response to their own faith and so they could not cope with what was before them.

It's amazing how often in church life, when a major step of faith is required, people will start to complain and discuss why it can't be done. They rely on the leaders' faith to take them through. Everyone rejoices in the miracle as they see that faith rewarded, but the majority have only been observers and not participants. When the next test occurs the same process is repeated instead of a corporate response of faith to move forward with God.

Paul is at pains to point out to us the sort of people the children of Israel were. It's easy to think of them as a poor bunch of peasants who had little intelligence and a rebellious spirit. We can easily picture them as a great rabble in the wilderness, a far cry from our sophisticated Western church life. However, Paul says to us, 'Don't be ignorant, don't be stupid.' These people were into miracles. They'd seen the Red Sea part, which is more than most of us have! They'd experienced the most extraordinary miraculous power of God. Six days a week they got up to find the ground covered with food. Every Friday there was twice as much as on any other day, and on the Sabbath there was none. This had gone on day after day after day. They never had to sow, they never had to reap. Food was provided on the ground every morning. On other occasions meat had been provided. Quails flying overhead stopped and dropped in for a meal! God provided for them most miraculously.

Water had come out of a rock, as if from nowhere. Their clothes and shoes never wore out. Can you imagine having clothes and shoes that continued year after year after year? Wouldn't that be a miraculous thing if it were to happen today? These were miracle people. As we read through the book of Exodus we see the most amazing interventions of God. We may think that today we're into signs and wonders and miracles, but these people saw things we have never seen.

Paul stresses that the disaster which took place among this group of people was to a miracle people. It's too easy and too dangerous to say that today we are exempt because we are into signs and wonders; we speak in tongues, we believe in ministry gifts, we understand prophecy and all the other wonderful things that happen in the church. It's too easy to believe that because we've seen these things we will be all right. Paul is saying that it is to just such people that the danger comes.

And let's face it—in so many situations today, in the midst of some very real blessing and signs of new life, we see churches struggling, torn apart by internal arguments and splits. This is happening in many places. If ever this warning was appropriate, it is now. Of course, we need to fight the enemy, but we will also need to be sure there is real repentance and change of heart if we are going to close the door to his work.

Although it must be true that so much of the harm we see is the work of the enemy, the destruction brought upon the children of Israel was an expression of the judgement of God upon them. Although he may have used negative forces to destroy, it was the Lord himself who allowed it to happen. He was so determined to have a pure people that he had to get rid of all that was opposed to his ways to prevent even greater harm to the company of people in the future. Sometimes God has to allow people to leave churches to prevent something worse happening later. The grace of God, of course, always allows for repentance and forgiveness. Often times, when sin comes to light, it is a part of the cleansing process, because if it were to go undetected it would always be an unseen barrier to God's work through that body of people. There can either be repentance and reconciliation, or if not then sometimes it is the grace of God towards the church that people leave.

Before we look in greater detail at some of the issues that caused the downfall of this great company of God's people, it would be helpful to mention something of the nature of the warfare.

11

The Spiritual Battle

Most of us appreciate that the church is engaged in a tremendous spiritual battle. The term 'spiritual warfare' is not mentioned as such in the Scriptures, nor is much of the terminology we use today concerning the subject. Paul, however, pointed out quite clearly to the Ephesians that they were engaged in a spiritual conflict. It was the final thrust of his letter to the churches in that region. He wanted to remind them that the battle they were engaged in was not with people, but with spiritual beings. We are very prone to seeing nearly all our problems in terms of people, because that is normally the way in which they present themselves. This means that we often fail to see the real power behind what is going on.

Although Paul was reminding Christians of their own personal battles, this letter was primarily written to the church and is about the church and therefore speaks to us of the corporate nature of this conflict in which we're engaged.

The battle for the church

The battle is on, and it is a battle for the church. It is the church that Satan hates and it is the church he wants to destroy. We are all involved in our own personal conflict with evil and we need to learn how to stand strong against the enemy. The Scriptures give us plenty of encouragements along this line. But it is the church that is the main target. It is difficult to know how to emphasise this strongly enough.

Jesus only spoke specifically about the church on two occasions, and on one of these it was in the context of warfare. (Although the term 'gates of hell' is not clear in its interpretation, the issue of conflict seems to be apparent here.) His commitment to build the church was in the knowledge that it would be engaged in a permanent struggle, but would not be overcome. We have seen in this century how evil forces have sought to destroy the church and remove its witness entirely from certain countries of the world. But when the curtain is lifted, we find the church has not been destroyed and in many cases comes out even stronger. The authorities of hell will not prevail against the church. But they will try. We spend so much time decrying the church and being embarrassed by it, that we forget what a tremendous threat it is on the earth to the powers of darkness. It is in the church that God has begun to re-establish so much of what the devil sought to destroy in the Garden of Eden. The church is a demonstration of the victory of the cross and resurrection.

The very presence of the church itself is a powerful weapon against the forces of darkness. No wonder Satan and his hoards want to destroy and break up the church. And equally we must work to see the church stay strong and growing in unity.

When Jesus was baptised in the Jordan and the Holy Spirit came upon him, he went out into the wilderness and was engaged in conflict with the enemy. From that time on, as he went about his ministry, he was continually engaged in conflict. He didn't decide to *do* spiritual warfare, he just was a battle zone wherever he went. As he walked around in the full authority with which he had been equipped and with the Holy Spirit working powerfully in him, dark forces exposed themselves and reacted to him whenever he met them. Just walking about he was engaging enemy forces. In exactly the same way, the church, by simply being the church, is itself a challenge to the enemy.

Light is always a challenge to darkness. As the church of Jesus preaches the gospel, prays, protests against injustice and is engaged in strong praise and spiritual worship, it will pose a threat to all that is evil. Jesus said, 'I will build my church and the gates of hell will not prevail against it.' As we allow Jesus to build the church, the powers of darkness will not be able to prevail. We will continually find ourselves involved in areas of conflict, and as we meet resistance from the enemy we are to fight and see him pushed back.

Now the church is always under enemy pressure. At the present time it may be comparatively light compared with pressure at times of revival. Observers will say that once revival starts to touch a nation, then the enemy concentrates his efforts onto the church. If we haven't learned to deal with the vulnerable areas and to understand the ways in which he works, then revival will not only be a time of blessing, but a time when churches may come under great pressure. We have the opportunity now to determine not to give him a foothold and to set up a guard against him.

Let's face it, even now we see the enemy running roughshod through the church. How many new churches have started out with such promise and hope, and are now shipwrecked by division and strife? They have to spend so much time sorting out internal problems that they have no time for the real business of rescuing men and women from the devil's clutches. If the enemy can keep the church looking at itself, he has little to worry about. Often we have provided so many footholds for him that he has no difficulty walking in and causing havoc.

Earlier in Ephesians Paul talks about these footholds for

the enemy. He speaks in chapter 4 of the times when we don't deal with anger. These, he says, provide a foothold for the devil. Weaknesses of the flesh, leading to sin, will always enable the enemy to have a foothold. If we do not learn to deal with hurt in the body of Christ, we continually invite the devil to ride roughshod through the church.

The children of Israel continually opened themselves up to problems. Paul is warning the church not to give the enemy the opportunity to walk all over them and to destroy their potential. We need to understand the seriousness of this. Churches are torn apart and spoiled because we are not taking enough concern over potentially vulnerable areas. We think we can get away with a few secret sins and it doesn't really matter if our behaviour isn't quite right. Every time we sin and fail to live the way God wants us to in our relationships, in our attitudes to one another and in our behaviour, we give a wide open door to the enemy.

I meet people who are behaving today in a way that is hurting them and their church, and the source of it is something that happened years ago. All the intervening time has provided an open door to the enemy. For example, living in self-pity or perpetual anger not only harms us, but everyone else as well. In the body of Christ, personal sin has corporate repercussions.

We cannot overestimate the power of the church in the battle for towns and cities. The lives of vast numbers of people depend on the church to be what it should be. We are not speaking here of perfection, as the church has always been made up of less than perfect people who are working out the reality of their salvation. We are speaking of taking away the footholds of the enemy so that the very presence of the living, united church will provide enough light to scatter the darkness.

This is why Paul writes to the Ephesian Church and tells

them how to protect themselves. We don't need to be primarily concerned with offensive warfare because if the church is acting properly it will, by its very nature, always be offensive. We do, however, need to know how to protect ourselves. Nearly all the teaching we hear today concerning the armour of God relates to the individual's Christian walk. This is probably because so much of our understanding of Christianity in the Western world is individualistic; much of our teaching is about personal faith and individual responsibility. But Paul was writing not only to individuals but to bodies of people—churches in Asia Minor. He was concerned not only for the personal spiritual battle but for the corporate nature of the battle. That's why he tells us to put on the whole armour of God. It is not just individuals who need to put on the whole armour of God, but churches. Paul is addressing church life and he is concerned that the church is protected from the attacks of the enemy. We must not only think about our individual walk with the Lord, however important that is, but see the vital importance of corporate life. If we neglect certain areas in our life together, we will be opening the door to the enemy.

My observation is that evil spirits seem to hop around churches from one person to another, if given the freedom to do so. Wherever they can find somewhere to put their feet they will go. Often you see a situation that has been caused through one individual; that is sorted out and then within a short space of time it arises somewhere else. It seems almost impossible to catch it as it goes from one place to another like a disease. Very often people who have been hurt at one time or another, and have not dealt with those hurts, have made themselves vulnerable to spirits to come and use them. This is particularly true of people who move from one church to another.

I've also noticed that where people are bitter, angry or

resentful because of something that has happened and another Christian comes alongside to help, they often get caught in the same problem. If they begin to get too sympathetic over the situation, they can take on board the same spirit. Of course we are to be loving and reach out to those who are hurting, but sometimes we can open ourselves up to the same spirit the other person is carrying.

If we do not retain some objectivity in the situation, but only feel what they feel, we can also receive what they receive. And so in the name of Christian love and care, our negative attitudes start to be spread around. This is where we need to learn to speak the truth in love to one another. We must go on loving and being compassionate, but we must also be honest and truthful. It is as important to speak truth into someone's life as it is to embrace their situation. Otherwise we may find ourselves not only hugging a person, but welcoming a spirit as well, in the sense that the same attitudes start to plague us too.

In Ephesians 6, by using the illustration of armour, Paul gives us clear guidelines as to the priorities in church life that will enable us to keep the enemy at bay.

1. Truth

He talks about the very foundation of our life being truth. How often do lies and half-truths go whizzing around the church? It's probably the fastest grapevine around and few people ever stop to find out whether things are true or false.

We must be absolutely ruthless with the truth and together determine certain ground rules of conversation. We must agree that we will not talk about a thing unless we are sure that it is true and that it is helpful. I have written later about the problems of gossiping and murmuring. If only truth and nothing but the truth were to be spoken in church life, what a difference that would bring about, not only in terms of keeping the enemy from the door, but also in terms of the reality of our Christian lives. Jesus spoke the truth and was the truth, therefore there was no foothold for the enemy in his life. Our lives, both corporately and individually, are so riddled with half-truth and unreality that we are sitting targets for trouble. Truth opens the door wide to the Holy Spirit for reconciliation, healing and power because he is the Spirit of truth. Lies open the door to the devil for division, suspicion and sickness because he is the father of lies. The decision as to which door is opened the widest is left to us. The belt was the foundation of everything else. The issue of truth in the church is not a peripheral one. It is the very foundation of church life together. If we understand this we will guard it jealously.

2. Righteousness

There must be such a priority on holiness that we close the door to all the filth and dirt that the enemy would want to bring into our lives. It is all too easy to become incredibly complacent about sin and we can find ourselves living at the level of what we can get away with. In the past, we have concentrated so much on minor issues, such as whether it is right to go to the cinema, parties, drink alcohol, own a nice car or smoke cigarettes, that we have forgotten the real issues of holiness that have to do with attitudes to one another, words we speak and our day-by-day behaviour. Sexual permissiveness is only one area where it is obvious that the concept of becoming a Christian seems to be divorced from an understanding of the kingship of Jesus in our lives. The fact that we can discuss whether it is possible to have Jesus as Saviour and not as Lord shows how far we may have come. Holiness must once again be seen not as a pietistic list of what we cannot do, but the glorious possibility of living the Jesus life in the power of the Spirit; and this life is not a life of withdrawal from joy and of being strait-jacketed, but the exact opposite—a life of real freedom.

The purpose of having small groups in a church should not only be to have good fellowship and to care for one another, but also to challenge one another in areas of righteousness. This could easily be misunderstood as creating places for criticism or self-righteousness. But often we cannot see ourselves as others see us. We miss behaviour in ourselves that is unholy, as we only see things through our own prejudiced vision. We need other people's help if we are going to live right lives. We must learn how to help one another bring the word of God to bear in our lives and encourage each other to live by the standards Jesus sets. In the Great Commission, Jesus told us we were to 'teach one another to obey'. If that is what he told us to do, that seems a good reason to do it.

3. The gospel of peace

The church which is always ready to share good news and sees that as a priority in its life will be one which is not continually looking at its navel and searching for problems. There is a world of difference between a stagnant pond and a flowing river. The picture in Ezekiel 47 of the river flowing from under the Temple is a wonderful picture of the church. Everywhere the river flows there is life. Any body of people which ceases to move forward will turn in on itself. Any group of people which loses the concept of an enemy without will start finding an enemy within. When we stop uniting together to fight the devil through preaching the gospel, we will turn round to fight one another. By concentrating on the proclamation of the gospel, we are continually reminding ourselves of the amazing grace of God by which we live, and our lives are challenged by the message we give to others.

4. Faith

It is a great shame that the word 'faith' has been spoiled for many of us by what has become known as 'faith teaching'. We have seen so many excesses of so-called 'name it and claim it' and 'prosperity' teaching, that it has put many off the whole concept of faith. Yet, as we look through the New Testament, we find we are consistently challenged to be people of faith. We are told that without faith we cannot please God. Church life must be full of corporate expressions of faith as we move forward with new challenges from God. It is possible that if we look at most of our churches, we would have to admit that a great deal of what goes on can be explained in human terms. If we were to look at the early church, even though we would have to say there was a lot of humanness about it, we would also see a great deal that would be impossible to explain except by acknowledging that God was around. It is a continual challenge to us to be trusting the Lord in such a way that if he does not act, we will be in trouble. It does not mean moving into foolishness, but it does require us to be risk-takers.

The choice is between being worldly, which is basically a denial of the presence and power of God being expressed in our attitudes and behaviour, and being full of faith, which means living our lives together believing in the God of the Bible who is alive today. If we took a few more risks we might be amazed at what God would do.

Faith in the corporate sense means that when the church is feeling the 'fiery darts of the evil one', it is able corporately to go to God for his protection and ask him to crush his enemies. It also means that when obstacles to moving forward are met, then there is an agreed attitude to believe God for miraculous intervention.

5. Salvation

The heart of the church's message must be salvation. It is interesting that it is described in terms of a helmet, as a helmet often denotes the identity of the army that you're fighting for or, in the modern world, the organisation you belong to. So many churches have been led astray because they moved away from salvation as their central message. Some very important issues have come our way which we have all needed to learn and think about, but when interests such as healing, inner healing, deliverance, concern for the poor, green issues, Israel and so on become central, we are in danger of being led down a side track. It is amazing how many good churches have taken up an important issue and then allowed it to become the total focus of their attention so that winning people for Jesus has been pushed to the side lines. The enemy has used a good and worthwhile cause to divert them from their prime call. If a church is known primarily for an issue it pursues or a doctrine it majors on, it is likely that it has been blown off course.

6. The sword of the Spirit, the word of God

Here is what rescues us and keeps us safe, as well as providing a weapon of attack. We must always keep as close as we can to the Scriptures. I realise that throughout the Greek text we find two words translated 'word'. The use of the word *rhema* here probably may not refer to the whole Bible as such, but to a particular scripture that the Spirit brings to mind in the time of need. This is best demonstrated by Jesus himself in the temptations in the wilderness. In order for this to happen, we must be well versed in the Scriptures.

Hasn't failure in the area of biblical understanding also been the means by which so many have been shipwrecked? A nice, exciting teaching comes along, given through such apparently godly and often miracle-working people, and we are taken in. The people we must be most careful of are those who are outside the context of the local church. If their teaching is not able to be tested by a local eldership, we need to be on our guard. The proliferation of tapes, videos and magazines is the modern way for the spread of dubious teaching. All tapes in circulation should carry a health warning. If you spread tapes around a church without checking them out with the pastor of that church, you may be guilty of introducing false teaching into the body. We must all be like the Berean believers who 'searched the Scriptures to see if these things were so'. We can never go far wrong if we are always asking, 'Where is this in the Bible?' It needs to be said, of course, that it often requires more than a superficial glance to really grasp what the whole of Scripture teaches. That is why God has put the gift of teacher in the local church.

'The Lord told me...I have this picture!'

We need to be rescued from the terrible syndrome of everyone blaming God for everything that goes on. It is all too easy to do something we want to do, and because we have a good feeling about it, we announce that God has told us to do it. The desired result, of course, is that nobody dares argue, because who wants to argue with God? My experience of knowing what God has said is that it seems to get less clear as you go on in life, which may mean that we become less dogmatic about it. Usually, when we are unsure, we speak out with even greater conviction that we know something to be God's will—maybe to help us overcome our doubt. Now, we should hear God's voice and know his will, but may I make a plea for a little more restraint before we make bold statements, or we may be attributing something to God that he has nothing to do with. At the end of the day, the test of Scripture has to be the guideline. For example, the young couple who told me that it was all right for them to sleep together before marriage because they were in love and they had prayed about it and the Lord had said it was all right, needed to be told they were talking nonsense. We may need a bit more courage in this area. I'm afraid that those who most want to be led by the Spirit are the most open to deception.

This may be a good point to mention 'pictures,' which I take to be visual prophecies. May I again make a plea that some people move on from pictures to giving full prophecy. What I mean by this is that often the picture gives you the starting point out of which to prophesy more fully. Such a lot of the pictures we have are the product of vivid imagination and the danger is that we can have the idea that anything which comes to mind is from the Lord. The worst situation is when someone has a picture which is so obscure, we all spend hours trying to work out what God might possibly be wanting to say. It is as if God is either struggling to make himself clear or else he is playing some rather delightful game with us which we can all join in on. Having said all that, let us not 'despise prophecy' but encourage as much of the genuine as possible, remembering that it will never contradict the Scriptures.

7. Prayer

As a final and fundamental guideline, Paul exhorts the people to pray 'in the Spirit on all occasions with all kinds of prayers and requests. With this in mind, be alert and always keep on praying for all the saints.' That's a pretty comprehensive sort of praying. In other words, he is saying that the secret of spiritual victory is to pray, and in our praying we will keep the enemy at bay. We remember how in the book of Nehemiah, when the people were continually under attack as they rebuilt the walls of Jerusalem, they worked out a strategy whereby some people would be ready to fight and some would build. Even the builders kept a weapon on them. Nehemiah described how he 'set a guard day and night'. If the church is going to be protected from the onslaught of the enemy, there will need to be a good prayer base for it.

It's interesting that the prayer Paul writes about here is primarily prayer for Christians. This is not the aggressive praying 'against the enemy' or for the lost, but it is praying for the church to be the church it is meant to be. In fact, the New Testament teaches us very little about praying against enemy forces unless we come across them in the ordinary pattern of things. It would appear that we are not to go looking for demons. They may come looking for us and obstruct our path in some way. It is then that we are to resist them. Even Jesus did not go demon hunting, but he did deal with them when he came across them. There is also very little said about praying for unsaved people. I am not suggesting that out of compassion and concern we should not pray for them, but it is not the main thrust of New Testament praying. Sometimes we would do better to pray for ourselves to be bold and then get on and talk to people rather than just praying.

Paul understood the dynamic nature of the church. He also understood the reality of the enemy who cannot be seen and the tremendous danger he is to the church. We cannot see the enemy of the church, but if we assume that 'out of sight is out of mind', we are heading for trouble. If we begin to understand the reality of this warfare, it enables us to understand many of the things that have been going on which we have previously put down to the activities of certain 'problem people'. How many more difficult situations would have been avoided if we had 'set a guard' in prayer?

It's interesting also to note that part of this prayer is for Paul, that he will have boldness as he opens his mouth and shares the gospel. This surely is a part of the warfare, the proclamation of the gospel in power. As we pray for the church and its defence, we are also to pray that there will be a fearless proclamation of the gospel which is the most aggressive and powerful form of spiritual warfare. When Paul went to a new city, his greatest means of engaging in warfare was to pray and preach.

Even when we have a concern for the gospel, it is often the case that we end up only praying for the lost when, in fact, it's power for the saints that is required. As we read about the new Christians in Acts 4, the great need for modern Christians is unusual boldness and confidence to share their faith. We should continually be praying for one another that we will have this boldness and that it will increase and become stronger.

We must pray with Paul that at the moment when we need it, we will be given words which are appropriate for every given situation.

Now to return to 1 Corinthians 10. Paul explains to the early church that the reason why stories of Exodus were recorded was not just so that they could be encouraged by all God had done, but primarily so that they would not make the same mistakes as the children of Israel and then suffer the same terrible consequences. In the next chapters, we'll take a brief look at some of those mistakes.

12

Idolatry

It's easy to assume that we know what idolatry is. It's something that the heathen do! In fact, idolatry is happening as soon as we put something else in the place of God. This is a constant temptation for all of us as we so readily look for a means whereby we can continue our self-centred living, free of God's control.

I often have to ask myself, 'What consumes my thoughts? What consumes my energy? What consumes my passion?' Whatever it is, that's my God; that's the thing I am worshipping. We may say we worship God, but whatever it is that consumes our passion, our thinking time, our energy—that is our god. This is true, however good the thing might be. Church and ministry can easily become idols. We must remember that we do not worship idols for what they are, but for what they can give us. They enable us to live independent of the true God and still provide all our basic needs in life. Everybody has a need for security, satisfaction, value. All these requirements for our lives should be provided by God so that we live in perfect trust in him.

People don't worship other gods because they think a particular god is worth their adoration, but because of what they believe the god will give them. They worship fertility gods because they want to be fertile, the sun because it gives light and heat, and so on. We are consumed with material things, relationships, success and the like because of what these things will give to us. We can pay lip service to God himself, but actually fill our lives with so many other things because they give us the freedom to be independent, as well as providing for our basic needs.

Dealing with idolatry in our lives means coming back to a real understanding of what it means to be a child of God and living in simple dependence upon him.

Paul makes it quite clear that idolatry was one of the main reasons why the children of Israel never entered the Promised Land. If we look more closely at this we may gain some understanding of what was really going on. Moses went up the mountain to receive the Ten Commandments and he stayed there rather a long time. He was the people's main link to God, and as they had failed to trust God for themselves, his absence must have made them very insecure. They needed something on which to centre their attention. They needed a visible representation of God and so they made a golden calf, or more likely a golden bull, out of the trinkets they had brought from Egypt. They melted them down and made a bull to worship. For us that seems an extraordinary thing to do, but where they came from in Egypt there had been the worship of Baal gods whose symbol was that of the bull. It was a visible, identifiable god. In Canaan, the land to which they were meant to be going, there was also a vast amount of idolatry, which again included the worship of Baal, symbolised by a bull. These were the gods of natural strength and fertility.

When times got really tough, the children of Israel reverted to their natural instincts. They must have found it so hard that Moses was asking them to believe in a monotheistic God whom they had never seen, while everybody around them could at least look on the gods they knew. In other words, they really wanted to be like everybody else, and that was the heart of their idolatry.

It wasn't just that they wanted to worship a piece of gold—I can't imagine they were that foolish after the miracles they had seen—but they did want to be like other people. They wanted some space away from this radical living and they wanted something they could see and touch. It is always easier to worship something you can see and touch. Worship of the living God requires such faith, and the personal rewards are not always immediately evident, it is so much easier to concentrate on the physical, attractive and immediate things around you.

It is always a tremendous temptation for all of us as Christians to back off from the Christian life which is an utterly radical form of living. To believe in a God we cannot see and in whom we are to trust for the provision of all our needs, and to understand the demands he puts on our lives, pushes us into a radical form of living. It is a lifestyle that is totally different from the way people in this world live. Many of us are not sure we want to be that radical. We don't mind belonging to the church and believing in God, but we're not sure we can take it to the limits. We really do want to have the things other people have, enjoy the same pleasures and share the same priorities in life. I want to be liked by the world around me and not be seen as someone rather odd. Similarly, the children of Israel must have thought, 'We'll be far more acceptable to the world around us if we also have a golden calf or bull to worship rather than an unseen God.' Strangely enough it was the very radical nature of a God no one had seen that was to cause such panic in their enemies and to enable them to conquer the people they encountered. But, at this time, they had a feeling they would be more acceptable by being like everybody else, without realising that this would never have worked.

In the world in which we live today many people are looking to the church to give an example of a lifestyle that is utterly different, and many feel let down by what they see. They do not want a church which looks like a slightly improved version of something they already have. They do not want a church which is rather like the local golf or tennis club, but instead sings hymns and listens to talks! They are looking for something which is utterly different.

The greatest temptation to every one of us as Christians is to conform to the pattern of the world around us and not to be different in the way we live. We're called to believe in a supernatural, all-powerful God who is Provider and Father, and we are to turn our backs on the temptation to be swamped with materialism and the pressures of the world around us that demand we become like everybody else. If the church becomes like the world in which we live, we'll never enter our destiny and we will fail to make the impact that God intends. We will never get to the end of our lives knowing we've fulfilled what God has for us. There is a corporate and a personal challenge in all of this. As individuals, we will just blend into our world and probably find that our faith becomes quickly dulled. As churches, we will wither away because there's no radical cutting edge. We have to be different from the world around us if we're going to impact our generation.

Let me make it quite clear this is not about the way we seek to communicate faith. Of course, in our communication, we must be relevant to our culture, but our standards, our behaviour and our values must demonstrate a radical difference from the world around us. Our separation from the world has nothing to do with getting physically alongside them or seeking to communicate by modern means. It has to do with a change of lifestyle and the way of thinking that lies behind this.

Some friends of ours came back from Africa recently

and made some interesting comments about the church in the country they had been to. They observed that although many people were becoming Christians, they brought their idols into the church and somehow found a compromise between their idolatry and their new-found faith. Our friends commented how different that was from the West, where we were able to take on Christianity without the trappings of idolatry. The tragedy is, however, that we have equally absorbed our idols into the church. Let me give you an example.

Consumerism

If we were to sum up the spirit of the Western world, we probably couldn't find a better word than 'consumerism'. It was suggested in one of the secular newspapers that this is probably the most self-centred generation there has ever been. This is the 'me' generation. In other words, everything in life is there to serve me and I must get as much excitement and fulfilment as I possibly can in the short life that I have. I can now choose what I want down to the finest detail, given the enormous variety of choice that is available. I can go from one shop to another, or one restaurant to another, and I can pick and choose until I find what suits my personal need. When it no longer suits me I can throw it away and get another one. We don't bother to repair things any more—they become obsolete, so we replace them. Relationships, including marriage, are treated in the same way. When this no longer pleases me, I discard it. My personal pleasure and satisfaction are of primary importance.

The tragedy is that the spirit of consumerism is deep in the heart of the Western church: 'The church is there for me, to provide for my needs and to help me become what I want to be.' Have you noticed how many people get tired of a church because it isn't meeting their needs, and then they find another one which looks really wonderful? When they arrive at their new church they comment to the leadership about their old church, which was so insufficient and inadequate and failed in so many ways to be what it should be. But they're so glad to be in this new church, because they see in it everything they hold dear. The leadership are flattered that their church is so wonderful, and they encourage the person to stay. Of course, two or three years down the line this church may be challenging that person in a deep point in their life, or something happens that causes them to begin to see that this isn't what they had in mind after all. And then, as before, they start to find things wrong with it. Fortunately, while they are complaining about the church they are now in, they hear of another one which really seems to fit the bill, so they decide to leave and go there. The tragedy for these people is that they may well go hopping from church to church for the rest of their lives. They will never actually be happy, because they are consumer Christians.

So much of the complaining and moaning that goes on in churches is because certain things are not meeting our own personal needs? Even Jesus becomes an idol. How many people enter the Christian life because they actually believe Jesus is there to meet their needs? Someone has told them that life is rather inadequate without God and that if they gave their life to Jesus he would sort it all out. He would then look after them, answer their prayers and be at their beck and call. All goes well for a time, until they find one day their prayers aren't answered. Things don't go the way they are planned. Life seems hard and God seems distant. Where is this Jesus who is meant to be like the genie in the lamp, always there to answer their requests? They find themselves disillusioned with Christianity. The truth is that what they picked up wasn't Christianity anyway, but an idolatrous form of it.

How many have become Christians because of a belief that Jesus would just give their life that little bit extra and be available to answer prayer when needed? Ultimately, Christianity is about our need of forgiveness and a call to serve God with our lives. We cannot come with any demands or with any expectations of what God will do for us. After all, we came to Christ because we desperately needed forgiveness and we were absolutely amazed that God would receive us at all. If we do not come back to God as the prodigal did, with the heart of a servant, we will never know what it is to be sons. We will always live immature Christian lives because God is always seen as someone who is there to meet our needs.

Of course God does meet our needs. Of course God provides for us. He is a loving, caring, heavenly Father. But our response to that should be undying gratitude and thankfulness, not a pursuit of our wants and rights.

It's extraordinary how worship has been tainted by consumerism, having become something that is there for our enjoyment. How often do you find yourself saying, 'I like this form of worship, but I don't like that form of worship'? It might be helpful for us to remind ourselves that actually worship is for God and it wouldn't do us any harm to ask what sort of worship God likes; as if we didn't already know that. He likes worship that is in Spirit and in truth. He's concerned with the heart and not with the method. But we're all caught up with whether it gives us a good feeling or not. We talk about powerful worship. Surely worship is an expression of our love for Jesus, whatever form that takes. But we are an experience-orientated generation. We must have higher and greater experiences. We love to go to events and hear preachers who do something even more sensational than the last one. Just to hear the word taught has become extremely dull for many.

We have got to be entertained with all sorts of amazing things as well.

Please don't for a minute imagine that we should not be looking for signs and wonders and miracles. Of course we should. That's a part of the gospel. But when we have to be entertained, we have totally missed what it is all about.

What consumerism creates within the church is a passive form of faith as opposed to an active form of faith. In countries where there is tremendous growth and revival taking place, their Christianity is active, whereas so much in the West is passive. This is particularly seen in five areas:

1. We serve when it is convenient

In an active faith we serve because we are part of the body of Christ and every part must function fully. This requires discipline, a servant heart and a desire to give our energies fully into fulfilling our own gifting and calling within the body of Christ. It means being willing to do menial tasks as well as the ones which receive acclamation. It means that we're in for the long haul as far as our service is concerned, and not just for a few months or a year or two until we get tired of doing that particular thing. Most areas of service are fine to start with and the novelty keeps us going for a bit. But then we find it isn't quite as interesting as it used to be and it's a bit monotonous, so we begin to enquire as to whether we could stop doing that and maybe find something else to do. Serving, of course, should never be a drudge if we're fulfilling the particular gift God has given to us. That's why it is so important in church life to make as much effort as we can to discover our spiritual gifts and to be functioning according to our strengths. There is never a place in the body of Christ for those who would just be passengers. Every part of the body must function, even if it's a small part, so it's reasonable to ask every member of the church what particular function they are fulfilling. When every person fulfils their part actively and with commitment, then the body can move ahead as it should.

2. Pray when we feel like it

In active Christianity, prayer is a discipline and a commitment. But so often in the Western church, where we are passive in our faith, we pray in a crisis or when it is extremely convenient. The thought of getting up early to meet with others to pray, to turn out to meet with the rest of the church to pray or to pray in small groups requires a great deal of discipline, which many of us are not prepared for. We're conscious that when we look at other parts of the world where the Spirit of God is moving powerfully, prayer is high on the agenda. In the West it is a minority pastime. That may explain why the church is so impoverished.

3. Giving without sacrifice

In active Christianity, giving has to do with cost and sacrifice. Although giving may appear to be generous in the passive church, it is rarely costly. It is an extraordinary thing that in poorer countries where God is working powerfully, there is such tremendous sacrificial generosity. Most of us who go into these countries are embarrassed by the overspill of generous hearts towards their visitors. It is common in the West to give, but to give out of our surplus. We have to make sure, first of all, that we have every luxury that we cannot live without and that everything else is taken care of, and then God gets the extra. The Lord is wanting a church that puts its money into extending the kingdom of God. If every believer gave a regular amount of money in proportion to their income (at least a tithe), as well as giving free-will offerings over and above that, there would be no shortages within the church. Then those para-church organisations which are of God could be funded out of local churches. They would be supported by local churches, especially if their function was to support the work of the local church. There would be no shortage of supply for these mission organisations that really are a service.

So many people want to argue about whether tithing is biblical or not, but often those people who argue are those who give even less than ten per cent. The first mention of tithing in the Bible predates the law and it came from the overflow of the heart. The overflow of a generous heart today surely would begin with ten per cent, unless your circumstances clearly disallow it. The best way to tell whether money has control over your life is to see how easily, or with what difficulty, you give it away. It's amazing how sticky our fingers are when it comes to giving. So many who do give still want total control over what they do with their money. If you are committed to a local church, that is where your money should go first of all. There is a desire for keeping control of our money that can just be a reflection of the individualistic, independent spirit so common today.

When the Holy Spirit fell on the early church, in the account in Acts 2 and 4, it is recorded that there was an overflow of generosity towards one another. They didn't consider that they were giving to the church, because they were the church. They just saw that what they had was there for the benefit of all and to help fulfil the vision God had given to them.

4. We meet together when we feel like it

In the active church, people follow the scriptural injunction not to neglect to meet together, but to come together whenever we can to encourage one another. In the passive church, gathering together is only for our convenience. Now, I don't for a moment want to suggest that church meetings are the centre of everything. We can get into a terribly driven state where we feel we have to attend every meeting, or we are not being obedient to Christ. But if we turn up to house group when we feel like it, or go to church gatherings when we just happen to be in town (or up in time), we become a source of discouragement to many. The body needs to meet together. We need to touch one another's lives. We need to find one another and encourage one another. We do not come to the church meetings primarily for our benefit, but we come to give to the Lord and to give to one another. But when church gatherings are only seen in terms of what we might receive, then if another place offers more we go off there. Whereas if we see them as a place where we come to give, then we will want to make sure that we take part as much as we possibly can.

5. We share our faith if we really have to

In the active church, there is a sense of, 'Woe is me if I share not the gospel.' It is something that is seen as part and parcel of the Christian life. It is just something that everyone does as often as possible. In the passive church, it becomes a mighty effort after training courses, much prayer and as a part of a special event, that we brace ourselves to find someone to tell the good news to. The first part of this book was devoted to this subject.

Conclusion

One of the reasons why these attitudes are so strong in the church is that we have fallen into the trap of only doing things as we 'feel led'. This is not necessarily the same thing at all as being led by the Spirit, but is much closer to being led by our feelings. Our feelings will always tend to go the way of least resistance and settle for what is easiest. The oppressive spiritual atmosphere in which we all live will also affect our feelings. It will cause us to shy away from doing anything we do not feel like doing. So we become increasingly passive in our lives.

If this is going to change, we must begin to make decisions and speak to ourselves. Undoubtedly, when we do, our feelings will change. If we are going to get up early to pray, and we say that we will see how we feel at 6 am, we are unlikely ever to get up to pray. But if we decide the night before that that is what we are going to do, we will do it, and we might even be surprised at how much we enjoy it. Decision often precedes desire, and desire may well lead to delight. The key to change lies in the will and if the will is weakened, everything is out of shape. When we determine things with our wills, it affects the whole of our lives. The early disciples (Acts 2) 'devoted themselves...'. This was no casual attitude to convenience, but a clear decision to be committed to Jesus, to one another and to the world. These were people of passion. We all have to learn to take ourselves in hand if we are going to break through.

Let me suggest that we all ask ourselves what decisions we have made in any of these areas. Then let us see if we are sticking to them. If not, then some changes need to be made. Let us not allow ourselves to get away with kidding ourselves that we will do it if we feel led.

Secondly, we must examine our attitude to church and

be sure we have not taken on board the consumer spirit. Some people may genuinely need to relocate, but let us be careful not to hop about, always demanding that *our* needs are met. It is a recipe for disaster.

13
Sexual Immorality

As soon as the children of Israel decided to compromise, they started to commit sexually immoral acts. The devil is using the same means today to destroy churches as he has done for generations. Sexual immorality is rife within the Western church. We hear of too many leaders who get into adulterous or immoral relationships and have to leave the ministry. There are churches where people within the leadership are found to be living immoral lives. All this has enormous repercussions on the whole church. How many in our churches are involved in adulterous relationships or are sexually permissive outside of marriage, and nobody knows about it? Many of us are aware of churches all over Britain and North America, as well as Europe, that have been destroyed because of immorality in the leadership and immorality among members. There is absolutely no doubt at all that if the enemy wants to destroy the church you are part of, he will try and use sexual immorality. It is highly unlikely that anyone who says they have never been tempted sexually is telling the truth.

If you're a normal adult person, you will have been tempted sexually in some way or other, and so will most of the people around you, including and especially your leaders. It is a common temptation for everyone because God has made us sexual beings. Temptation itself is not wrong. It is merely an invitation. What you do with the invitation determines whether you sin or not.

We live in an extraordinarily immoral generation. It appears that most of the boundaries have been removed. There are no longer any rights or wrongs about sexual relationships. The only guidelines at all are the fear of unwanted pregnancies, AIDS or in some cases the pain caused by committing adultery. Sexual relationships between unmarried people have become almost as common as dating. 'If it feels good, do it' has become the normal pattern for people today. Surveys that have been carried out suggest that a surprisingly high percentage of men have an affair at some point in their lives. Because adultery is usually done in secret, it involves a great deal of deception. If something of the world's standards has seeped into the church, then how much is going on that nobody actually knows about? The deception is being lived out by so-called Christians everywhere. *We* may not see it until it is disclosed, but God does.

There is tremendous pressure today on every side. The media, through advertising, comedy programmes and drama, press home the message that there is no moral reason why people should not do whatever they want to, and sleep with whomever they want to. Television rarely demonstrates the pain and hardship of immoral relationships, so although we are fed a diet of unreality, it affects us all very deeply.

It's easy for us adults to say to young people, 'I remember what it was like to be young.' We may remember, but it is a completely different issue to be a young person today. The temptations and the pressures are far greater than they've ever been.

The sad thing is that in so many of our churches the word 'sex' is never mentioned, except maybe as a dirty word. Yet everybody finds themselves thinking about it, and they are bombarded with it through all forms of the media, but especially television. Young people may be asking questions about it and yet hearing so little that is positive or true. If we really do believe that God invented sex and he made it such a good and important part of our lives, and if we recognise that it is also such a key area of temptation for all of us, then surely we really need to be teaching about it regularly in our churches. This way we can give it a positive emphasis such that when people see the good side of it they have stronger defences against temptation.

The best way to overcome what is going on in the world is not to scare people off, but to show them the positive and creative side of what God has made. Jesus has given us clear guidelines as to how we are to live, and with the gift of the Holy Spirit he made it possible for us to live that way. These are not impossible demands, but we must decide that they are the only standards by which we will live. If we don't make some vital decisions in our lives, we'll never get to the end of our lives with that sense of satisfaction that we ran the race and that we fulfilled the calling God had for us. What a tragedy that so many start out very well and yet fall because they never made positive decisions about their sexuality.

We must decide to be different from the world around us. The devil doesn't want us to fulfil our destiny. He will trip us up along the way and very often he will use our sexuality to do it.

We must be absolutely clear. Sex is a gift from God. Sex is for marriage, and marriage is for life. There is no place for sex outside of marriage. It is too good a gift to be spoiled. If we're following Jesus, that's the way we must live. There is no question about it and there are no alternatives.

When I recently spoke on the subject of sex, I was questioned afterwards by three young people. It was noticeable that they each repeated almost the same story: they were committed Christians, but were sleeping with their non-

Christian partners. It seemed strange that this was talked about as if it were fairly normal. It was not that long ago that non-Christians would have been embarrassed to have been found out having premarital sex. Now it is not even seen as out of the ordinary for the Christian young person. Each person said that if they broke off their sexual relationship, they would probably lose their partner and that it would affect their partner's future commitment to Christ. Interestingly enough, all three chose to change their behaviour, and two of the partners became Christians in a very short period of time afterwards, both admitting that they knew it was wrong all along. The third lost her boyfriend, but testified that the moment she stopped, she was aware of God's presence in a way she had not known before.

The greatest pressure today is the pressure on leadership. These are the people the devil will really go for. This is because if he can compromise them, he can bring the whole church into disrepute. It is also true than most leaders are more vulnerable that anyone else. Surely if we want to see the church strong, we will pray for our leaders and provide help for them so that they will not get into a compromising situation. They are, of course open to temptation in the same way everyone else is. They are subject to the fantasy world of television, the imperfections of marriage, the attractiveness of relationship without commitment, the pressures of bringing up children and the inherent weaknesses of the flesh. As well as all this, they are under far greater pressure from the devil than most people in a church situation. Let me mention some of the things which make them very vulnerable.

1. Loneliness

To be a leader is often to be a lonely person. This is not the leader's fault; it is more a consequence of this position. It's very difficult to have many close friends within the church you are leading. It causes slight tension in a relationship if you are both leader and friend. This is not to suggest for a moment that friendship is not a good thing within the church. It surely is, but the reality is that it's often quite difficult. Most leaders will tell you they suffer terribly from loneliness. So often they receive the criticism, but not any praise. They are making decisions, often on their own, and feel unsupported by those around them. They live continually with the tensions as well as the joys of church life, and the responsibility never goes away. They don't close the office door at 5 pm and go home.

Loneliness leads to the need for intimacy and if things are not brilliant at home, they may be open to the attentions of someone who offers care and understanding, but does not demand commitment. The neglect in recognising female leadership often isolates husband and wife in the church arena. The wife feels an appendage and unable to be who she was made to be, and she is forced into the role of 'leader's wife'. This can leave her very alone and unfulfilled. The husband takes the pressure alone and is equally vulnerable. What a disservice has been done by not encouraging husband and wife teams to operate. The truth is that the average church member has no idea of the particular pressures on church leaders, nor of the great loneliness that can be caused. Leaders are usually people in need of real friends.

2. Insecurity

Many leaders are desperately insecure. There are many who have a good platform ministry and seem totally together when viewed from a distance, but in themselves feel incredibly insecure. We have placed such expectations on those in full-time ministry, that there is a pressure to perform and come up with the goods week after week. As many actors are insecure and hide behind their roles, so preachers and teachers can hide behind their pulpits and their polished sermons. They have often been taught theology, but have little or no knowledge of how to handle people. Rarely does a congregation stop and help a pastor come to terms with his or her gifts. They are confident in their area of strength, but still vulnerable when people will not release them from having to perform in the area of their God-given weaknesses. These areas then need to be covered by others.

3. False expectations

So often expectations of leadership are far higher than can be achieved. I often feel sorry for Moses. He was always the butt of all the complaints. The people blamed him for everything that went wrong, but they never seemed to give him any credit when all went well. He had had no previous experience of leading a million or more people round a desert and had not read any books by people who had done it before. He had not volunteered for the job. All he did was stop and look at a burning bush and the rest, as they say, is history!

The expectation to get it right all the time, to know exactly what God is saying, to be an expert in everything and to never be allowed to make a mistake puts a lot of pressure on leadership.

4. Family pressure

The nature of church leadership often leaves families under a great deal of pressure. The job does not run from nine to five, so there are often demands on the leader's family that are not required of others. Frequently this is because of poor teaching for leaders on how to organise their lives or how to make sure the family gets a good look in.

When a number of these things are working in a person's life, it makes them very vulnerable to another person who comes along and appears to understand, gives tenderness, love and acceptance, and is not demanding in any way. What can start out as a very innocent relationship of support and care can easily drift into becoming a sexual relationship that will destroy a marriage, a ministry and often a church.

What leaders need so much are good friends and open relationships. They need people who will talk to them and find out how they really are. They need close friendships with people who will challenge them about their family and areas of vulnerability. They need people they can go to when they are feeling tempted and to share that with them. If it's true that every one of us will be tempted (and that this will be particularly true of those who are in leadership), then we need to build in the safeguards. It is incredibly important that everybody has some opportunity to share with someone else with whom they can feel totally secure. Where would you go if you had a strong sexual temptation and you wanted someone to talk to? Is there someone in your life to whom you have given that privilege? I have found in my own life there are times when I have really felt the pressure and I've rung up a friend and said, 'I need to talk to you and I need you to pray for me.' It's a great help because sexual temptation is nearly always deceitful. You tend to keep it to yourself and then it grows and eats away at you. As soon as you begin to talk to somebody else the pressure goes. Sexual sin is nearly always accompanied by the feeling that 'this will never get out of hand, I am in total control...' so look for the escape route. All sexual temptation has an escape route early on, and the difficulty comes because we so often fail to take it.

We must close ranks on the devil over this whole issue of immorality. We cannot allow the standards of the world to become the standards of the church. We must teach and talk about sex as much as we need to in order to give clarity about God's pattern, but also to help one another. We need to avoid bringing condemnation on one another, but to see that we are all struggling in the same areas and need to help one another through the difficult times.

Whatever church you are in and however godly your leaders appear to be, if they are human beings they are vulnerable to sexual temptations. Do not be naive enough to look out on all the lovely looking people in your church and feel, 'All is well here. These nice people would not entertain such thoughts.' Remember, 'Let him who thinks he stands, take heed lest he fall.'

It will happen to you unless you admit that it could and begin to build in the safeguards. Remember this: there is only one thing to do when faced with sexual temptation... run. Take the example of Joseph and get out of there fast. That was the advice of Paul to Timothy. Cut out all the clever stuff—the discussion as to what you can cope with and the limits you can go to. If you see any possibility of it coming, run as fast as possible. If you see anyone else anywhere near getting into trouble, grab hold of them and warn them.

Fire is a wonderful yet dangerous thing. In a fireplace it provides warmth and heat and a wonderful sense of peace. Out of the fireplace, it can be frightening and devastating in its effect. Sex in marriage is a wonderful thing. Out of marriage, it has the potential to do enormous harm. Make no mistake about it, this is the central theme of so much of what is going on around us, in conversation, thoughts and actions, and if we as a church ignore it, we do so at our peril and everyone's loss. We owe it to a lost world to show them that there is real hope. We do that by the way we live and by what we say. We are to live out lives of purity and to speak of sex, not in hushed whispers or with embarrassment, but with joy and freedom as we talk of a wonderful gift of God to humanity.

I cannot close this section without saying that for those who have fallen and messed it up, the grace of God is always sufficient. There will always be scars, but God's forgiveness and healing are always flowing to those who admit their failure and are willing to start again. What would we do without the love of God? The church is also to be a place of restoration and healing for those who have failed.

In summary, we must help each other in these matters. Silence will cause secrecy and guilt. Make sure you are helping someone else and they are helping you.

Prayer shield

It would be foolish to end this section, having referred to struggles that leaders face, without saying that a lot of trouble may be diverted if leaders were being supported in prayer. We have so often failed to understand that leaders face a greater level of enemy attack than others. If the enemy can bring a leader down, the damage is far greater and wider in its effect than for other people. In his excellent book, *Prayer Shield*, Peter Wagner unpacks this whole issue. He presents a very convincing case for every leader to be sure to be surrounded by a number of people who pray for him or her regularly. All leaders would do well to take this seriously if they want to be there at the end of the race.

14
Murmuring

When you read the account of the children of Israel in the wilderness, you quickly become aware that the people complained on a fairly regular basis. At every major crisis they seemed to murmur and complain. To be honest, some of the conditions weren't exactly perfect. After all, if you lived on manna for breakfast, lunch and tea every day for forty years, you might think that life was a bit monotonous. These people were living out in the wilderness in tents. It was hard going. In many ways some of their conditions weren't as good as they had been back in Egypt. There were a number of things they could genuinely complain about. But of course in the midst of this they had an enormous amount to give thanks for. They were a free people, no longer under bondage and slavery. God was providing miraculously for them every day. They had evidence of his presence right in the middle of the camp in the tabernacle, the pillar of fire and the cloud. But still they managed to complain. It's amazing how rosy the past can seem when we're in a place of trial and difficulty. We seem to have extraordinarily short memories and forget what life was really like. The children of Israel were no exception to this.

Now it is quite apparent that when the people complained against Moses concerning the conditions they were living under and the tests of faith they had to face, they may have appeared to be complaining against Moses, but in reality their complaint was against God. And this is at the heart of the sin of murmuring. That was why God treated their murmuring and complaints with such severe punishment. God's response to it seems, at first sight, to be out of proportion to what they had actually done; he destroyed thousands of people, purely because they complained. The reason is that all complaining is ultimately against God. It is an open denial of the love and care of God and his abundant provision for his people. It is a challenge to God's love and justice. It is also true that those who murmur cause a cancer in a body of people. If it is not dealt with, it is extremely destructive.

Ultimately, every complaint we have is a complaint against God if we really believe that God is in control of our lives. This applies not just to complaints within the context of the church, but in every area of our life. The truth is that none of us has enough of what we want. We often find it easier to fix our eyes on people who are better off and have more things than we do. It's always easier to look to greener pastures and complain, instead of looking to the multitudes who are worse off and being thankful for what we have.

When we travel to Africa or other poorer parts of the world, it's amazing how it changes our attitude to life, at least for a few weeks after we return. Suddenly we become aware of how little other people have and how remarkably they exist on it. Coming back into the West we are aware of the extraordinary abundance in which we live. It certainly stops us complaining for a time, but it's astounding how quickly we forget. We are faced with the reality of it on television week after week. We're aware of how poor so much of the world is, yet we complain. And every complaint is against God. Even in the extraordinary abundance of the Western world, we have the audacity to turn around and complain that we don't have enough.

If we believe that God is our Father and he loves us and he is an all-powerful God, our complaints deny what we say we believe. It is a denial of the love of God for us. It is a denial of God's fatherhood.

So often Christians quote the verse 'all things work together for good for those who love him and are called according to his purpose' (Rom 8:28 AV). If it really is true that all things are working together for good, then that must apply to those things which are apparently hard, as well as those things which are apparently easy. If the bad things and the good things work for good in our lives, why is it that we complain? Oh, I know we say that it isn't quite as easy as that, but in fact it is. Anybody can complain and murmur, because there are always things to complain about. But it is a challenge to us to make sure that what comes out of our mouths is positive and creative.

However, murmuring is more than just complaining. The very word itself conjures up a sense of something running and moving around. And that's what murmuring does. It moves about, creating disturbance, unease and unhappiness. It runs from one person to another, often making people who have no complaint realise that things are not quite as good as they ought to be.

Let me make it absolutely clear that it is vital in church life to have constructive criticism of things that go on. If we ever get rid of that, we are in a very dangerous situation. If we end up with an authoritarian form of leadership that will not listen to any form of criticism, then we are in for trouble. If we disagree with things or are unhappy, we must speak out, but we must speak to the right person. If we bring a complaint to anyone except the person it concerns, we are in danger of being destructive. We must understand that murmuring is quite different from disagreement. If we disagree about something, it means we've thought about it and we basically do not share the same view as someone else. That's not a reason for leaving a church or undermining a leadership. There's plenty of room in every church for people who do not agree. In fact, it can be a very healthy and stimulating thing. We can still support the basic direction of the church and encourage and get behind the leadership, even if there are some areas we disagree on. That may well be part of the richness of church life. In fact, some people who disagree with something may keep quiet, assuming it is wrong to comment, and the person with whom they disagree misses out on the benefit of what they have to share. Nobody has the total monopoly on truth and a wise person listens to good criticism. For example, most preachers would do well to welcome and ask for creative criticism. Although we are all vulnerable to being criticised, if we want things to improve, we must listen to helpful comments. This is true in every area of church life. Nothing is going to be perfect, but most things could be improved by positive, creative criticism.

Murmuring is another thing altogether, even if it has some of the same content. Murmuring is usually related to drawing wrong conclusions from facts received and these are then spread around. The content usually undermines someone's character and puts another person in a bad light. Its motive, its tone and the means by which it is disseminated cause it to be destructive and undermining. It creates gossip and negative talk. We must understand that murmuring and complaining are so serious that if we allow them to be part of our lives, we may never fulfil God's purpose for us personally, and we may destroy the purpose of the church. Be absolutely sure of this: you will die 'in the wilderness'. You may even cause the church to die in a wilderness. If it is a complaining, murmuring church, it will never fulfil God's plan. This is very serious stuff. This is no joke. Thousands of people were destroyed by snakes in the wilderness. And the church opens a wide door to the snakes, the enemy powers, as soon as it allows murmuring to spread. You may think you have a just cause; that what you are saying is true. You may feel you are only saying these things to a few friends 'in confidence'. You believe that what you are doing is harmless. But God hears and God sees, and he knows that your complaint is ultimately against him.

It is worth noting that so often our complaints concern people's weaknesses, as if it were either wrong or surprising that people have areas of weakness. If any of us did not have weak areas we would not need anybody else and we would not need to be a part of a body. Our strengths are a gift from God. Our weaknesses are a gift from God. He made us with certain talents and he expects us to use them fully for him. He does not demand that we shape up in areas of giftedness that he did not give us. If we complain about another person's weakness, we complain about the way God made them. If we are unhappy about another person's behaviour, we shouldn't murmur about them behind their back, but go and tell them to their face. Instead of destroying them, we may even rescue them. Most murmuring of that kind is done out of pride and arrogance. It is the equivalent of saying, 'Of course, if I were in their position, I would never have behaved like that.' Pushing other people down is often a subtle way of pushing ourselves up. God obviously hates this sort of behaviour. Don't you think we should too?

Murmuring can often begin with quite small things, but quickly becomes a pattern of life. You may start murmuring about the way the meetings are led, the way the chairs are put out, the songs that are sung or some decision that the leadership make. Whatever it happens to be—however small or large the matter in question is—it will ultimately be aimed at some person or other, but when you start murmuring about other people you are actually complaining against God. This is a huge problem in the church today. If we could only become more aware of our common enemy, we might just begin to stop looking at one another and criticising everything. It's as if we need someone to fight and if it isn't the devil, it will be other people in the church. Murmurers (uncannily close to the word 'murderers', isn't it?) are usually frustrated people. They have not been able to get their way in some area or other and so they begin to act out of hurt. They provide a stepping stone for the enemy to do his destructive work of lies and slander.

Let me say something about hurt at this point. As I have mentioned earlier, the need to deal with hurt is of prime importance in our lives, both personally and corporately. If we believe it is possible to be in a church and not at some time get hurt, we are naive. The church is made up of a bunch of saved sinners trying to get their lives sorted out. They have dared to say that it is possible to live at a deeper level of relationship than most people have been able to in the world today. Put those two factors together and you get the inevitable result of misunderstanding, hurtful comments and thoughtless actions. Things are said or not said and in our insecurity we get hurt. This is to be expected. Why else did Jesus teach so much about forgiveness? He knew we'd have to do a lot of forgiving. Seventy times seven may not be far from the mark! If we cannot forgive one another (and let's face it, it is easier to write about than do), then we'd better forget about being church. If we can learn forgiveness, and learn to sort things out quickly and not let them fester, we will save ourselves so much trouble and pain. Most major crises in church life are the final explosion after a long build-up of difficulties. If we can defuse situations as we go along, what trauma will be prevented!

Paul says that he wants to warn the church. We cannot afford to be casual about this issue of murmuring which so often is built on a foundation of hurt and self-righteousness. It is said that the Moravian Church had a pattern of living whereby if someone came to you and started moaning about someone else, then you had a commitment to take hold of that person and lead them straight to the one they were complaining against and have them speak out their complaint there and then. How that must have sharpened the mind! It certainly would have cut down the moaning, so maybe we would do well to bring it into our church life.

I do believe God wants to fill our hearts with thanksgiving. We live in abundance, and it is time we stopped moaning and murmuring and complaining about the nitty gritty little problems of life, and decided instead to rejoice in all we have. We need to turn our behaviour around and do the opposite of murmuring, which is to give thanks and look at everything we have, every blessing we have, and say thank you to Jesus for allowing us to have all of this. We need to look at the church's life, look at the leaders, look at those around us and begin to look with eyes of thankfulness. We need to look for the positive things and the things we can be grateful for. There are always going to be negatives and positives in any church. But we are faced with a choice: we can either murmur and complain about the things that upset us, or we can turn and give thanks for what is good. Whatever choice we make, we will either be a source of blessing or a source of curse. We will either open the door to the Holy Spirit, or we open the door to the enemy.

It needs to be said that all of this is made much easier if we have leaders who listen and are open to examining themselves, are accountable to others and are prepared to admit mistakes. Sometimes leaders do not help the situation by remaining unmoved by the very real problems folk are facing, and this can create frustration. People do not usually mind being disagreed with, but they do like to know that leaders have listened to them.

Finally, if you have been the source of unrest or have spoken unkindly, go and put it right. You must certainly confess to God, but it may be a good thing, on occasion, to confess to the wronged person. It might even strengthen the relationship in the long run. You must also be willing to admit to those you have talked to that you were out of line. Confession is a great source of healing.

Make an agreement with your friends that you will check each other against destructive talk. Then, when someone starts to say, 'I know I shouldn't say this but...' you'll be able to interject with, 'Well don't!'

15
Treachery

One day some of the members of Moses' leadership team came to him with a spokesman by the name of Korah (Num 16). The basic content of what he had to say to Moses was: 'How come you're the big shot around here? Are you really the only one who can hear from God? What about us? Why shouldn't we be leaders as well alongside you? What makes you so special? We don't want a Number One person—we all want to lead.'

It seems utterly reasonable, doesn't it? I'm sure it can be heard all over the place today. God, however, didn't think it was reasonable. His response to this 'utterly reasonable' suggestion is recorded as such: 'The ground under them split apart, and the earth opened its mouth and swallowed them, with their households and all Korah's men and all their possessions' (vv 31-32).

God didn't think the situation was very funny. In fact he saw it as extremely serious. What could have evoked such a violent reaction? These people were undermining and destroying God-given leadership. And this is a very serious issue. There is a place for challenging ideas, for questioning decisions, for arguing, for discussing in depth the direction of church life with those God has called into leadership, but there is never a place for undermining and usurping God-given leadership in the church.

Now there may be some fundamental questions that

every church leader should ask, and the first is: 'what is my prime gift?' There are many people who are pastors, but they are not leaders. They need to be responsible for the pastoral care of the church, but they are not visionary leaders. Others are quite clearly leaders and visionaries, but not very able when it comes to pastoring or teaching. Every leader of a church needs to sit down with those around him whom he can trust and really be honest about his gifts and calling. When it is decided that a person has the call of God on his or her life to lead a body of people, then that must never be undermined or destroyed.

Why have we seen so many church splits over the past years? It usually begins with a challenge to the leadership. Rarely does anyone stand up and oppose openly. It often begins with someone who gets the ear of a number of folk who are, at least, a little disgruntled. They have very reasonable differences with the present leadership and begin quietly to voice them, sharing with people they know will agree with them. They are merely a spokesperson for a growing body of people. Most of this goes on behind closed doors without being heard publicly.

The same spirit that was in Absalom is not uncommon in the church today. It is the desire not just to disagree with, but to challenge and remove God-ordained leadership. The final confirmation of the evil nature of this is that when it comes to a head and there is a division, they leave, taking a crowd with them, usually those they have already won over to their point of view. The mark of the godly man is that usually, if he has to leave, he leaves alone because he does not want to harm the body. The one who does not mind destroying a church leaves with his followers. There are, of course, exceptions to this. In the past, when the leadership of a church have been closed to the work of the Holy Spirit, it has caused such frustration that many have eventually had to go if they were ever going to move for ward in their Christian lives. The main area of problem is caused not by cases like that, but by people who are deliberately undermining leadership in the body. When we create this sort of open door to the enemy, it is no wonder we experience so many church splits.

In the Old Testament, these accounts were very dramatic and it may be tempting to think that they do not matter so much today. We are not aware of massive judgements on the church as there were on the people in Moses' day. But let's face it, the church in the West is not exactly prospering today, is it? Maybe judgement takes on another form. God in his mercy may spare us from the same type of consequences, but does that mean God has changed his attitude? If we fear the Lord, then we will be very careful how we behave—not because we are afraid of punishment, but because we do not want to grieve him. The Western church is in danger of being very casual and needs to get back to being more in awe of God. Our behaviour shows up how shallow our experience of God is. We claim to know him, but our behaviour speaks volumes about the sort of God we say we know. We pray for the revival power of God, but that brings with it a profound challenge to our attitudes and behaviour.

There has been strong reaction over past years against the whole practice of one-man ministry. This is quite right, as God has given the ministry to the body. There will be some with more clearly defined ministry gifting than others, but the work of ministry is for the whole body of Christ. We are told in Ephesians 4 that the whole purpose of certain gifts to the church is so that they can equip the whole church to do the work of ministry.

The difficulty is that we have confused the plurality of ministry with the plurality of leadership. So many places have moved into group leadership in their church life. Many are now finding this is causing great problems, especially as the church begins to grow.

The Bible teaches that leadership is a gift. It may be that different people receive different levels of leadership gift appropriate to the different areas in which they are to exercise that gift, ie, house group, youth work, children's work and so on. Eldership is not exactly the same, as the calling is based upon character and not so much on a specific spiritual gift. The recognition of elders will be on a different basis than purely spotting the gift of leadership, although most of those who are called to do the work of an elder will have leadership gifts. Leaders need to make themselves accountable, but the church was never meant to be a democracy, and it never will be. God has appointed in the church those with the gifts of leadership and they are called to lead. They are not meant to set themselves up as mini-gods or tyrants, but they are to come with a servant heart and a willingness to lay down their lives for the flock. Most leaders are only too aware of their own weaknesses and insecurities, and often find that there are many people around them who seem to be more naturally gifted in certain specific areas than they are. This can easily make them feel threatened. What leadership needs more than anything else is encouragement, friendship, support, prayer and honour.

In fact one of the things the Bible says is that leaders are to be honoured financially. This is a rarity in the church nowadays, where most leaders are kept on a very tight rein financially and therefore feel controlled by the church. They are made to feel that as they were appointed by the church they are also owned by the church and therefore must basically do what they are told. Leaders expect to be led by God. Leaders are not there to be the puppets of the people—they are there to lead the people. Moses didn't lead the children of Israel by consent. He heard from God and he shared it with the people.

My observation is that God speaks to the people who need to hear. If you are in charge of the Sunday school work, the likelihood is that the Lord will speak to you about the Sunday school work and it will be confirmed by other leaders. If you are the overall leader of the church, God will speak to you about the direction of the church. What is amazing is how many people are seeking God for direction, when God has not given them the calling or the gift in that area. Many people obviously believe that God will tell them where the church is to go and what the church is to do, but he won't have told the leader, so they have some obligation to go and tell the leadership what they should be doing. Of course, any leader who hears something from God will check it out if he has any sense at all.

He will talk to people. He will share it and see what the response is. If it is from God, the likelihood is that it will be confirmed both by prophetic word and also by the hearts of other leaders and by the people. If you seek God for a word or for guidance in some area that is not your responsibility, the likelihood is that you will be deceived. There are large numbers of people in churches who are being deceived because they are seeking God on issues that do not concern them. They then become manipulative and controlling, and ultimately, if they don't get their way, they can become undermining. They will go around saying, 'The leadership do not listen to me.' The truth is the leadership will not do what they say. If God continually entrusts the direction of the church to someone other than those in leadership, that person is either a prophet or, from God's point of view, must be the leader!

I know that the fear in all of this is that we may end up with dictatorial leaders. We are in fact much more likely to get the job done if we respond to strong leadership and give them all the support we can. A far greater danger is that would-be power seekers will come to take over the church and drive out the leadership. People like this are ultimately divisive because they are aiming to demonstrate their own power, and when they get into a position of control the church may suffer serious consequences. If they are not allowed to have the control they want, they usually break away. Because they usually take others with them, they show that they are divisive, destructive people who have no love for God or for the church of Jesus Christ. That may sound rather strong and harsh, but we do need to take these issues seriously.

In fact, the advice given by one leader—'Never appoint elders in the church until the church has faced at least two major crises'—may well be very sound. It is only in a crisis that you discover people's real motives and loyalty. If they are still around after a crisis and show themselves godly within it, they are likely to run the course and can be trusted through other stormy times that may arise.

In the new church scene today, there is much freedom for people to get involved in many different areas of church life. The new freedom carries with it great dangers. The majority of church splits and divisions today take place in new churches. It would seem that with greater freedom come more opportunities for abuse. Because many of these churches have been struggling with the whole concept of leadership, and because they believe so strongly in plurality of leadership, they are now finding it difficult to use any other model because it causes tensions within the body. Churches that have clearly defined leaders seem to move forward with far greater purpose. If we appreciate that God gives vision and direction to leaders, and this may be one person or a couple, supported by a team, then our responsibility is to use our gifts as best we can to serve that vision. There is absolutely no point in a church trying to serve a whole lot of people with different visions.

'Obey [be persuaded by] them [your leaders] so that their work will be a joy, not a burden, for that would be of no advantage to you' (Heb 13:17). Are you a source of joy or burden to your leaders? Please answer this question before you read on. It is too important to skip over. If you do not know the answer, I suggest you go to them and ask them.

Conclusion

> These things happened to them as examples and were written down as warnings for us, on whom the fulfilment of the ages has come. So, if you think you are standing firm, be careful that you don't fall! No temptation has seized you except what is common to man. And God is faithful; he will not let you be tempted beyond what you can bear. But when you are tempted, he will also provide a way out so that you can stand up under it (1 Cor 10:11).

Let us pray with all our hearts for the revival power of God to sweep through the church and the nation, and let us heed the warnings and determine to close the door to the enemy who seeks to destroy the church. At the end of the day, let us be found 'standing up', victorious.

A Warning and a Promise

In the book of Exodus, we read of the remarkable deliverance of a whole nation from slavery and bondage. It is accompanied by amazing demonstrations of God's power on behalf of his people. But the story is, in the main, a tragedy. This same group of people failed to enter their destiny. Not because God let them down and failed them at the final hurdle, but because they failed to be the people God wanted them to be. He simply wanted a people who trusted him. They started off so well and finished so sadly.

Then God gave them another opportunity. He had to wait for another generation before he could accomplish what he wanted for and through them. But he made a promise to them and as they stepped out again in obedience to his word and with the promise ringing in their ears, once again the waters parted and the road of faith opened up before them. They proved that they had many of the same weaknesses as the previous generation, but at least they were willing to press forward and enter the land God had prepared for them.

And what of this generation? We live at a time of unprecedented moves of the Holy Spirit across the world, but we cannot live on other people's blessings. We must listen to the Spirit's call to us in our own situation and our own generation. We are aware of the darkness and the hardness everywhere, but we also hear the promise. It is a promise of revival. It is a promise of land to be taken. It speaks of things that only God himself can do and yet of things that will not be done without the co-operation of men and women. We are people under a promise; the promise of Scripture that as we move forward, he himself will be with us, and also the promise of present-day prophetic words encouraging us of an outpouring of the Spirit, which will result in an enormous harvest of people being swept into the kingdom of God.

How should we then act? It must be with faith, but with faith comes risk. The call to be strong and very courageous can only be intended for those who have the potential to be discouraged and lose heart. In the midst of all that would dishearten us, the Lord's call on us is surely to 'pull our tent pegs out of the ground', put away our tents and move forward onto unfamiliar and yet God-given ground.

This will be a time of strong and hard warfare. Take the warnings to heart or we will see still more destruction in the body of Christ. Who wants to be on the wrong end of the judgement of God or provide an opportunity for the devil to devour the flock?

However, moving on means leaving behind. In order to experience the fresh move of the wind of the Spirit, we will have to move from where we are, and it may be costly. The hearts of tens of thousands of men and women are waiting to be won to the kingdom of God. The time has come for us to say that whatever it costs us, we are going to do everything we can to make that possible, knowing that in the end, all power comes from him.

We are faced with the choice of staying where we are in the relative comfort and safety of what we have and what we have known, or risking everything for a higher prize. The church must put the needs of a dying world before its own desires, or there is no hope.

We are faced with a choice.

Scripture encourages us: 'You are a chosen people, a royal priesthood, a holy nation, a people belonging to God, that you may declare the praises of him who called you out of darkness into his wonderful light' (1 Pet 2:9).

The moment the church fails to put the proclamation of the gospel as its main priority, it ceases to be relevant to its generation. Let us not lose sight of our calling.

Lightning from heaven

The promise of spiritual awakening has sometimes been described in terms of lightning striking from heaven. Lightning will strike the point that gives it the best contact with earth. The people of God who are in touch with heaven but who are also seeking to touch their world will surely provide a good place for divine lightning to strike and to go on striking.